PAUL R. FRIEDMAN is Managing Attorney of the Mental Health Law Project, a Washington, D.C. public-interest law firm which has spearheaded the legal-reform movement on behalf of mentally retarded and mentally ill persons. During the past five years he has been involved in such landmark cases as *Wyatt v. Stickney* (the right to treatment), *Donaldson v. O'Connor* (the right to liberty), *Souder v. Brennan* (employment rights), *Roe v. Doe* and *Whalen v. Roe* (the right to confidentiality of mental-health records), and *Bartley v. Kremens* (civil commitment of mentally handicapped children). Mr. Friedman is the author of "Mental Retardation and the Law: A Report on the Status of Current Cases," which has been published quarterly since 1972 by the President's Committee on Mental Retardation, and co-author with Bruce Ennis of *Legal Rights of the Mentally Handicapped*. He has written numerous articles and lectured widely on such subjects as legal regulation of enforced therapy in institutions, the problems raised by institutional labor, the right to treatment and the right to protection from harm, and the mental-health law and public-interest law movements generally.

Mr. Friedman is a research candidate at the Baltimore-District of Columbia Institute for Psychoanalysis; a fellow at the Center for Law and Social Policy; and a member of the American Psychological Association's Commission on Behavior Modification, and of the Secretary of Labor's Advisory Committee on Sheltered Workshops.

Also in this Series

Where better paperbacks are sold, or directly from the publisher. Include 25¢ per copy for mailing; allow three weeks for delivery.

Avon Books, Mail Order Dept., 250 West 55th Street, New York, N.Y. 10019

AN AMERICAN
CIVIL LIBERTIES
UNION HANDBOOK

THE RIGHTS OF MENTALLY RETARDED PERSONS

THE BASIC ACLU GUIDE FOR THE MENTALLY RETARDED PERSONS' RIGHTS

PAUL R. FRIEDMAN

General Editors of this series:
Norman Dorsen, *General Counsel*
Aryeh Neier, *Executive Director*

 A DISCUS BOOK/PUBLISHED BY AVON BOOKS

AVON BOOKS
A division of
The Hearst Corporation
959 Eighth Avenue
New York, New York 10019

ISBN: 0-380-00868-8

First Discus Printing, December, 1976

DISCUS TRADEMARK REG. U.S. PAT. OFF. AND IN
OTHER COUNTRIES; MARCA REGISTRADA, HECHO EN
U.S.A.

Printed in the U.S.A.

Acknowledgments

I would like to thank Professor Richard Allen, Mr. Wallace Babington, Ms. Ronna Beck, Dr. James Clements, Professor Gunnar Dybwad, Mr. Robert Gettings, Professor Michael Kindred, Mr. Ray Nathan, Dr. Philip Roos, Dean Burton Blatt and Judge Joseph Schneider for making comments and suggestions which were helpful to me in writing this book. Susan Weiss of the National Association for Retarded Citizens provided an especially helpful critique.

Much of the information in this book has been put together during my tenure as managing attorney of the Mental Health Law Project. Needless to say, I am indebted to Patricia Wald, Bruce Ennis, Charles Halpern and other colleagues at the Project for stimulating me to research, think through and sometimes litigate the issues discussed here. I would also like to acknowledge the financial assistance of the following foundations, all of which have contributed to the general operation of the Project: the Edna McConnell Clark Foundation, the William Randolph Hearst Foundation, the Grant Foundation, the Eugene and Agnes E. Meyer Foundation, the New York Foundation, the Rockefeller Brothers Fund, the van Ameringen Foundation, Inc. and the Veatch Program of the North Shore Unitarian Church (L.I., N.Y.).

My research for this book has also been supported in part with Federal funds from the Department of

Health, Education and Welfare under contract No. HEW-100-75-0114, which supports the quarterly publication "Mental Retardation and the Law." The content, however, does not necessarily reflect the views or policies of either the Department of Health, Education or Welfare or of the Mental Health Law Project.

A resource of great value to me was the recently published *The Mentally Retarded Citizen and the Law*, (Kindred, et al. eds.) published by the Free Press.

Susan Fox and Jamie Kilbreath provided research and indispensible assistance in source-checking this manuscript, respectively. Finally, I thank my secretary Susan Winders, and, before her, Debbie Brown along with Phil Christopher for cheerful typing and proofing of many drafts and Lee Carty for skillful editing.

Paul R. Friedman
June 1976

Contents

Preface

This guide sets forth your rights under present law and offers suggestions on how you can protect your rights. It is one of a continuing series of handbooks published in cooperation with the American Civil Liberties Union.

The hope surrounding these publications is that Americans informed of their rights will be encouraged to exercise them. Through their exercise, rights are given life. If they are rarely used, they may be forgotten and violations may become routine.

This guide offers no assurances that your rights will be respected. The laws may change and, in some of the subjects covered in these pages, they change quite rapidly. An effort has been made to note those parts of the law where movement is taking place but it is not always possible to predict accurately when the law *will* change.

Even if the laws remain the same, interpretations of them by courts and administrative officials often vary. In a federal system such as ours, there is a built-in problem of the differences between state and federal law, not to speak of the confusion of the differences from state to state. In addition, there are wide variations in the ways in which particular courts and administrative officials will interpret the same law at any given moment.

If you encounter what you consider to be a specific abuse of your rights you should seek legal assistance. There are a number of agencies that may help you, among them ACLU affiliate offices, but bear in mind that the ACLU is a limited-purpose organization. In many communities, there are federally funded legal service offices which provide assistance to poor persons who cannot afford the costs of legal representation. In general, the rights that the ACLU defends are freedom of inquiry and expression; due process of law; equal protection of the laws; and privacy. The authors in this series have discussed other rights in these books (even though they sometimes fall outside the ACLU's usual concern) in order to provide as much guidance as possible.

These books have been planned as guides for the people directly affected: therefore the question and answer format. In some of these areas there are more detailed works available for "experts." These guides seek to raise the largest issues and inform the non-specialist of the basic law on the subject. The authors of the books are themselves specialists who understand the need for information at "street level."

No attorney can be an expert in every part of the law. If you encounter a specific legal problem in an area discussed in one of these handbooks, show the book to your attorney. Of course, he will not be able to rely *exclusively* on the handbook to provide you with adequate representation. But if he hasn't had a great deal of experience in the specific area, the handbook can provide helpful suggestions on how to proceed.

Norman Dorsen, General Counsel
American Civil Liberties Union

Aryeh Neier, Executive Director
American Civil Liberties Union

The principal purpose of these handbooks is to inform individuals of their rights. The authors from time to time suggest what the law should be. When this is done, the views expressed are not necessarily those of the American Civil Liberties Union.

Foreword

Mentally retarded citizens traditionally have been cared for under an "alms" model of services. Habilitation, education and employment were "favors" to be granted by legislators or administrators. The mentally retarded had no effective recourse when such favors were denied. Recently, however, lawyers and other advocates representing mentally retarded and otherwise mentally disabled persons have made a systematic effort to articulate and implement the statutory and constitutional rights of this historically neglected minority group through litigation, legislation and administrative reform. As a result of some landmark legal decisions, mentally retarded persons have come into their own as citizens, viewed as "consumers" rather than as "alms seekers." Actions on their behalf have aimed to stop abuses of their civil rights and to improve the services available to them. The administrators of the institutions and other programs for mentally retarded persons no longer have unreviewable discretion to grant or deny favors. They are now understood to be ordinary bureaucrats whose powers are clearly limited and who are accountable for their decisions.

Society used to forget about mentally retarded persons after they entered institutions (attending only to issues of admission and release). Now public scrutiny is being extended to all facets of the delivery of service within institutions and to the full spectrum of rights within the community at large.

While other books in this ACLU handbook series are addressed directly to the persons affected, few mentally retarded persons will be able to read and understand even an intentionally nontechnical book like this one. Therefore, this book is addressed to families and friends, to concerned professionals and to interested citizens, to help them become more aware of mentally retarded persons' rights and able to assert these rights more effectively.

However, the statutory rights of mentally retarded persons vary widely from state to state and the gap between what the law now says and what it should say is often still very great. Most persons wishing to assert specific legal rights of mentally retarded individuals must therefore depend upon the research and advice of lawyers with a special interest in and knowledge of mental-retardation law.

Unfortunately, the legal profession has historically been as unresponsive to the needs of this minority group as has the rest of society and it is still difficult (although, thankfully, becoming less so) to find lawyers with appropriate expertise. Appendix C lists both legal-service and consumer-representative organizations which are dedicated to protecting the legal rights of mentally retarded persons and which are available for consultation. If you contact the organizations near you, they should be able to help you themselves or to make an appropriate referral to someone who can. Alternatively you might take this book to your local private or legal-assistance or ACLU-chapter lawyer, pointing out relevant chapters and footnotes to give that lawyer a start. While you may still need great perseverance, the chances of finding sympathetic and competent legal representation on behalf of a mentally retarded person are greater today than ever before.

Introduction

BACKGROUND ON MENTAL RETARDATION

Although there are many different definitions of mental retardation, there is general agreement that a diagnosis should be based upon multiple criteria, including measured intelligence, adaptive behavior level and medical classification.[1] According to the definition which has been developed by the American Association on Mental Deficiency and which is widely accepted in the field, "Mental retardation refers to significantly subaverage general intellectual functioning existing concurrently with deficits in adaptive behavior, and manifested during the developmental period."[2] Thus, under this definition, performance on a standard intelligence test at or below an I.Q. of 68 is considered essential—though not sufficient—for such a diagnosis. Additionally, such subnormal intellectual functioning must be coupled with significant difficulties in adaptive behavior before a diagnosis of mental retardation is appropriate.

The emphasis on "deficits in adaptive behavior" under modern definitions of mental retardation makes it clear that mental retardation is a product of interaction between individual capabilities and social demands. A person can be "cured" of mental retardation by "improving" his functioning *or* by changes in the social demands made upon him.

13

A person is mentally retarded when "we" say he is. Mental retardation is not a fact, but a label or classification applied to a very diverse group of people—often for purposes of segregating or restricting them, although sometimes for purposes of providing services not available to all in the community.

More than 250 causes of mental retardation have been identified to date. Mental retardation may follow or be associated with infection and intoxication (e.g., rubella or syphilis); trauma or physical agents (e.g., encephalitis due to prenatal or post-natal injury); disorders of metabolism or nutrition; gross post-natal brain disease; chromosomal abnormalities (e.g., Down's Syndrome); premature birth; and environmental influences (e.g., lack of proper mothering, lead poisoning).[3] Yet in many cases, no specific cause can be determined. Clearly, considerably more study and research are needed.

Thus, mental retardation is a general label which refers to the results of a multitude of possible conditions, all of which have the common effect of significantly reducing an individual's intellectual and adaptive functioning. Levels of mental retardation vary from extreme impairment, rendering the individual practically helpless, to relatively minor impairment. Under the most widely accepted scheme, persons are classified as "mildly," "moderately," "severely" or "profoundly" retarded, based upon their degree of deviation from an average person's level of functioning.[4] *The gap in intelligence and functioning between the more profoundly mentally retarded and the mildly mentally retarded is greater than the gap between mildly mentally retarded and "normal" persons.*[5]

A widely accepted conclusion regarding the incidence of mental retardation in the United States is that 3 percent of the population (or more than six million Americans) will at some time in their lives function in the mentally retarded range.[6] This figure has, however, been criticized by some experts as erroneously high. Probably no more than 1 percent of the population, or two million Americans, are technically mentally retarded at any given time.[7] The peak period of identification is between the ages of 6 and 12 and such identification usually occurs after the age of 8 or 9.[8]

Significantly, about two-thirds of the individuals diagnosed as mentally retarded lose this label during late adolescence or early adulthood.[9] The school child's diagnosis as "mentally retarded" is later discarded, either because it was based upon culturally biased intelligence tests or because low I.Q., while it may pose a major handicap to success in formal academic environments, will have only a negligible or minor impact on the grownup's functioning on the job or in other out-of-school contexts. Since a diagnosis of mental retardation requires a lack of adequate adaptive functioning, and since adaptive functioning will vary with the nature of the tasks confronting the mentally retarded person, such persons lose this diagnosis when they leave the school system.

According to the President's Committee on Mental Retardation, slightly more than 275,000 people are institutionalized in the nation's public and private residential facilities for the mentally retarded, and there are waiting lists for almost all of these institutions.[10] Moreover, there are approximately 21,000 people labeled as mentally retarded (or almost 10 percent of the total prison population) in our prisons.[11]

In the past, most people thought all mentally retarded persons were severely or profoundly retarded. This misconception led the public to believe that most mentally retarded persons had to remain in institutions for their entire lives. In fact, the situation is quite the opposite. Today, as a result of massive public-education efforts by such groups as the National Association for Retarded Citizens and the President's Committee on Mental Retardation, the public is coming to recognize that, of persons with I.Q.'s approximately 85 or less (which includes "borderline" mental retardation), the significant majority are in the borderline or mildly retarded range while only some 5 percent are severely and profoundly retarded.[12]

While some of the profoundly retarded may have to remain in some form of sheltered custody during their entire lives, almost all are capable of learning and growth. Moderately retarded persons can be taught to take care of themselves physically and can learn some manual skills and perhaps master some formal school work. Mildly retarded persons can often achieve fourth-grade academic competency.[13] Moreover, mildly retarded persons are capable of economic self-sufficiency, and moderately retarded persons can be productive in sheltered employment. Approximately 95 percent of mentally retarded persons have the potential to be economically productive in our society.[14]

Traditionally, the mentally retarded have been viewed, without factual basis, as:

—subhuman organisms lacking many of the needs, aspirations and sensitivities of other human beings;
—menaces to society because of their criminal tendencies or because of their wanton reproduction of defective children;
—eternal children doomed always to be much younger than their age; or
—irreversibly diseased persons whose condition is hopeless and who can only be assigned to indefinite custodial care.[15]

The once-popular concept of "custodial care" was predicated on the assumption that mentally retarded persons were incapable of development. Inevitably, this became a self-fulfilling prophecy. But although these old myths of mental retardation are still widely believed, they are gradually being replaced by the developmental model: a recognition that mentally retarded persons are capable of growth and learning regardless of their level of retardation or age.

The developmental model is based upon the assumption that all human beings are in a constant state of flux and growth. It further recognizes that although the general sequence of developmental stages is sequentially established, environmental variables, both physical and psychosocial, can significantly alter the rate and direction of individual development and can enhance mentally retarded persons' human qualities, their ability to engage in complex behavior and their ability to cope effectively with the environment.[16]

A critical issue in adapting the developmental model to habilitation and training for mentally retarded persons involves the criteria to be used in selecting the rate and direction of the changes sought. While survival is, of course, the ultimate goal of all living things, it can be defined either as simple "preservation of life" or as "effective coping with the environment." Under the first definition, the goal of survival has often led to removal of as much risk as possible from the environment of mentally retarded persons. But in the second context, steps are taken to enable the mentally retarded person to cope with his environment as effectively as possible, thereby increasing his reliance upon his own resources for survival. Experts favor this latter definition of survival on the grounds that when a person is provided with more protection than he needs, he is diminished and becomes dangerously dependent.

Obviously, however, if retarded persons are offered as much autonomy as they are capable of, this will include the possibility of failing—just as everyone else enjoys this possibility. The "right to fail" (not so much a legal right as a human right) links the developmental model to the normalization principle. The normalization principle has recently been defined as: "Utilization of means which are as culturally normative as possible, in order to establish and/or maintain personal behaviors and characteristics which are as culturally normative as possible." [17] The normalization principle suggests that mentally retarded persons should live like nonretarded persons to the greatest extent possible, since the deviancy which justifies discrimination against mentally retarded persons can be reduced by minimizing the degree to which they are treated differently from others.

LEGAL RIGHTS OF MENTALLY RETARDED PERSONS

Mentally retarded persons in our society suffer denial or infringement of a wide range of basic rights.

Mentally retarded persons who are confined to institutions necessarily suffer infringements on their fundamental right to liberty and on many other constitutional rights which depend upon liberty, such as the right to travel, the right to free association and the right to privacy. Once committed, mentally retarded persons are often subjected to other deprivations, including denial of their right to medical treatment, to habilitation, to education, to autonomy, to privacy, to sexual expression and even to protection from harm.

In the community, mentally retarded persons are all too frequently deprived of fundamental rights enjoyed by "normal" citizens, including the right to education, to enter into a contract (to marry or even to buy a television set "on time"), to be licensed (for such diverse activities as driving a car or being a barber), to buy insurance, to vote and to be free from discrimination in securing suitable employment and housing. Discrimination against mentally retarded persons may deprive them of virtually all of their legal rights.

The plight of mentally retarded persons in the criminal justice system is perhaps even more desperate. Regardless of guilt, mentally retarded persons often confess to crimes because they are particularly vulnerable both to threats and inducements and to a desire to please. Moreover, a mentally retarded suspect who is charged with a crime often cannot understand the charge, cannot tell his side of the story and cannot help his lawyer to defend him. If, as often happens, no one realizes he is mentally retarded, his chance for a fair trial is gravely hindered. If convicted and confined, the mentally retarded person is often prey for other inmates and is usually denied the opportunities for education and habilitation which would allow him to conform to socially required norms in the future.

An important step was taken toward recognition that the mentally retarded person is entitled to basic human and constitutional rights when the United Nations General Assembly adopted the *Declaration of the Rights of Mentally Retarded Persons*.[18] Under this declaration, the mentally retarded person is given the same rights as other human beings "to the maximum degree of feasibility." He is also given the rights to "proper medical care and physical therapy and to such education, training, rehabilitation and guidance as will enable him to develop his ability and maximum potential," and "to protection from exploitation, abuse and degrading treatment." Unfortunately, the rights set forth in this declaration, as well as in position papers of consumer and professional groups,[19] and the statutes and court decisions discussed in this book are only just beginning to make a substantial impact on the lives of many of the mentally retarded citizens in our country.

The legal rights of mentally retarded persons may arise under the Constitution of the United States, under Federal legislation and regulations such as the Rehabilitation Act of 1973, the Education Act, the Developmentally Disabled Assistance and Bill of Rights Act and the Fair Labor Standards Act; under state constitutions, many of which, for example, provide a guarantee that the public education system will be "equally open to all"; and under state legislation and regulation in such areas as civil rights, employment and public housing. This book gives the reader an overview of the rights of the mentally retarded both as they are today and as they should be under the Constitution. The emphasis is on rights defined in court cases based on these constitutional and statutory protections.

NOTES

1. *See* Roos, "Basic Facts About Mental Retardation," in 1 *Legal Rights of the Mentally Handicapped* 17 (B. Ennis & P. Friedman, eds., 1973) [hereinafter "Roos"]. The discussion which follows draws heavily on Roos's excellent summary.
2. *Manual on Terminology and Classification in Mental Retardation* 5 (Amer. Ass'n on Mental Deficiency, Spec. Pub. Ser. No. 2, H. Grossman, ed., 1973).
3. *See* Hughes, "Definition, Diagnosis, Classification and Associated Problems in Mental Retardation," 1 *Law & Psychology Rev.* 17, 20-21 (1975).
4. Traditionally, the correlation between these levels of retardation and performance on the revised Stanford-Binet I.Q. test has been given as follows:

Current Retardation Term	Revised Stanford-Binet I.Q.
Mild	68—52
Moderate	51—36
Severe	35—20
Profound	below 20

But since I.Q. is only one of the multiple criteria necessary for a finding of mental retardation, determining mental retardation on the basis of I.Q. alone—which ignores the whole issue of adaptive behavior—is *not* condoned by current professional thinking.

5. It is important to note that the dividing line between "dull-normal" or "borderline" intelligence and mental retardation is an arbitrary matter, depending upon the demands of a particular society. As a society increases in complexity, fewer of its members are able to adapt to it successfully. Hence the number viewed as "retarded" is likely to increase.

6. *See* Roos, *supra,* note 1, at 21.

7. Letter from Dr. Burton Blatt, Director, Division of Special Education and Rehabilitation, School of Education, Syracuse University to Dr. Gunnar Dybwad, The Florence Heller Graduate School for Advanced Studies in Social Welfare, Brandeis University, November 6, 1975, suggesting that the incidence is 2 to 2½ percent. Neither figure includes persons classified as "borderline." If this borderline group were to be included in the class of mentally retarded persons, the class would be expanded to include approximately 16 percent of the total population.

8. Roos, *supra,* note 1, at 21. Also Blatt, *supra.*

9. *Id.*

10. Haggerty, Kane & Udall, "An Essay on the Legal Rights of the Mentally Retarded," 6 *Family L. Q.* 59, 62 (1972).

11. *Id.*

12. Roos, *supra,* note 1, at 20.

13. Letter from Dr. Burton Blatt to Dr. Gunnar Dybwad, *supra,* note 7.

14. Roos, *supra,* note 1, at 20-21. Moreover, as Dr. Burton Blatt (*supra,* note 7) notes, under modern habilitation approaches, even the remaining 5 percent of severely and profoundly retarded persons can be expected to live in community placements and, albeit not as fully self-sufficient workers, can still be seen as economic assets in that they will not cost the state hundreds of thousands of dollars for a lifetime of full institutionalization.

15. Roos, *supra,* note 1, at 21-22.
16. Roos, McCann & Patterson, "A Developmental Model of Mental Retardation," paper presented at 1970 Annual Convention of National Association for Retarded Children.
17. W. Wolfensberger, *Normalization* 28 (1972).
18. G.A. Res. 2856, 26 U.N. GAOR Supp. 3, at 73, U.N. Doc. A/8588 (1971).
19. *See, e.g.,* Appendices D and E.

I

The Problems of Classification

What are the consequences of being classified "mentally retarded?"

The adverse social consequences of being labeled "mentally retarded" have been documented in numerous studies. For example, a 1969 study [1] of American attitudes toward those labeled "retarded" revealed that more than half of the people felt that institutionalization is best for the retarded. In the same study, only 16 percent of those interviewed felt that mentally retarded persons should be permitted to work side-by-side with others. While a recent Gallup poll conducted for the President's Committee on Mental Retardation showed a marked improvement in willingness of the public to live in the same community and to work in the same office with mildly or moderately retarded persons,[2] the label "mentally retarded" still stigmatizes its recipient and may be a rationale for denying the retarded person the right to an individualized evaluation of his real assets and limitations.

Our society still has very little tolerance for any form of deviance. Failure to conform to highly valued cultural norms of intelligence, self-sufficiency and physical attractiveness may cause mentally retarded persons to be both viewed and treated as less "human" than others. That mentally retarded persons are viewed

23

as subhuman or menacing or as diseased or the objects of pity causes them to be isolated from many aspects of community life and denies them the right to a normal human existence. Moreover, mentally retarded persons subjected to stigma often suffer from lowered self-esteem, which in turn often results in retreat from challenge and avoidance of situations in which they (often incorrectly) expect to fail. This negative "self-fulfilling prophecy" aspect of classification as "mentally retarded" is one of its most fundamental and tragic consequences.

In addition to the negative social consequences of being labeled "mentally retarded" there are also important legal effects, both positive and negative. For example, special educational services may be available to a child certified as mentally retarded, but the school system may use this same label as the basis for excluding a child from the school system. Vocational-rehabilitation services may be extended to those labeled mentally retarded, but the same label may be used to prohibit persons from securing various licenses necessary to practice specific occupations such as barbering or driving a taxi. A person labeled mentally retarded may be excused from responsibility in a criminal suit, but the same label may prevent him from serving as a juror or entering into a legal marriage contract, or may be used by authorities as the justification for taking away his or her child.

Is there a right to due process before a person can be classified as "mentally retarded?"

Yes. Because the consequences of being labeled mentally retarded can include commitment to an institution, with its massive deprivations of liberty and of a variety of other rights and privileges, due process requires that such classification be accurate. At a minimum, this means that persons subject to being labeled "mentally retarded" have the right to procedural safeguards in the classification process. Furthermore, persons who may be classified as mentally retarded have a right to assessment instruments and criteria which are both fair and accurate (substantive due process). Labeling of persons as "mentally retarded" on the basis of I.Q. tests alone is notoriously inaccurate, both because I.Q. is only one of several factors necessary to an accurate diagnosis of mental retardation and also because I.Q. tests themselves have been shown to be biased against cultural and racial minorities.[3]

The 1974 amendments to the Education of the Handicapped Act require states receiving funds under that Act to:

> "provide procedures for insuring that handicapped children and their parents or guardians are guaranteed procedural safeguards in decisions regarding identification, evaluation and educational placement of handicapped children including, but not limited to (A) (i) prior notice to parents or guardians of the child when the local or State educational agency proposes to change the educational placement of the child; (ii) an opportunity for the parents or guardians to obtain an impartial due process hearing, examine all relevant records with respect to the classification or educational placement of the child, and obtain an independent educational evaluation of the child . . . and (C) procedures to insure the testing and evaluation materials and procedures utilized for the purposes of classification and placement of handicapped children will be selected and administered so as not to be racially or culturally discriminatory." [4]

Also in the right-to-education area—but this time through test-case litigation rather than legislation—

members of minority groups whose primary language is not English have argued successfully that equal educational opportunity involves the right to be free from inappropriate educational classification and placement. In *Larry P. v. Riles,* for example, black children classified as mentally retarded secured a court decision that a low score on a culturally biased intelligence test does not provide, in and of itself, a justifiable basis for classifying a child as "mentally retarded." The court enjoined future psychological evaluation by the use of culturally biased tests and placement of black children in schools for the mentally retarded on the basis of such tests.[5]

The kinds of substantive and procedural protections required by the 1974 amendments to the Education of the Handicapped Act and by the case of *Larry P. v. Riles* are not, of course, limited to the education area. Persons are entitled to these same safeguards whenever the possibility that they will be classified as "mentally retarded" is likely to have adverse consequences.

Another important aspect of the due process right to fair classification is the right of persons threatened with the stigma of being labeled mentally retarded or of their advocates to examine their records for accuracy and to be assured that the private details of their diagnosis and programs will be kept confidential.

Does it make sense at all to classify persons as "mentally retarded?"

Probably not. As has been explained in the introduction, the group labeled "mentally retarded" is by no means homogeneous. Rather than a universal statutory definition of mental retardation, statutes are needed which define persons or groups of persons functionally, for the purpose of regulating a *particular* activity. Instead of a global assessment device like the I.Q. test, different criteria are needed for assessing deficiencies in specific areas of functioning.[6] For example, many mentally retarded persons are perfectly capable of managing their personal affairs and of marrying. Others are not. (Of course some nonretarded persons in our society also have difficulties as personal managers and as marriage partners.) But under some laws, *all* persons labeled mentally retarded are automatically prohibited from marrying, even though many would be able to fulfill the responsibilities of this relationship.[7] Given the stigma which inevitably attaches to the label "mentally retarded," it would be best to avoid this label altogether and to determine competency to perform particular functions on grounds of actual ability, instead of relying on vague medical or psychological classification schemes. The same criticisms apply not only to the label "mentally retarded" but also to other related labels such as "incompetent," "trainable" or "noneducable," "dangerous," and even to such euphemisms as "slow learner" and "exceptional child."

NOTES

1. Roper Research Associates, Inc., Summary Report of a Study on the Problems of Rehabilitation for the Disabled (U.S. Department of Health, Education and Welfare, 1969).
2. "Public Attitudes Regarding Mental Retardation," prepared for the President's Committee on Mental Retardation by the Gallup Organization, Inc., Dec. 3, 1974.
3. Moreover, persons (especially children) with physical impairments (e.g., deafness) and/or emotional disturbances are too frequently misdiagnosed as "mentally retarded."
4. Education of the Handicapped Amendments of 1974, Pub. L. No. 93-380, §614 (Aug. 21, 1974), codified at 20 U.S.C. §1413(a)(13) (Supp. IV, 1974). The 1974 Amendments also require states to provide procedures to protect the rights of children whose parents

are deceased or otherwise unavailable. *See id.* §1413(a)
(13)(A)(iii).

5. *Larry P. v. Riles,* 343 F. Supp. 1306 (N.D. Cal. 1972),
   aff'd, 502 F.2d 963 (9th Cir. 1974) (preliminary injunction); Supplementary Order, December 13, 1974.
   See also Lebanks v. Spears, 60 F.R.D. 135, 138-141
   (E.D. La. 1973) (consent decree).

6. *See generally* Steinbock et al., "Civil Rights of the
   Mentally Retarded: An Overview," 1 *Law & Psychology Rev.* 151 (1975).

7. *See, e.g.,* Iowa Code Ann. §595.3 (Supp. 1975-76).

II

Overview of Civil Commitment, Competency and Guardianship Proceedings

RIGHTS IN THE CIVIL COMMITMENT PROCESS

What kinds of facilities are there for care and habilitation of mentally retarded persons?

A spectrum of habilitation services has been developed for mentally retarded persons. A mentally retarded individual should be provided with the services most appropriate for him in the most normal environment suitable to his needs (*e.g.*, a supervised-living situation or a nursing-care facility or a decent, humane institution).

The experience in Nebraska provides a good example of a statewide effort in the development of comprehensive community-based services. Massive and innovative changes in traditional mental-retardation services have occurred in a relatively short period of time. As late as 1968 there were only two alternatives in Nebraska for parents of mentally retarded persons: institutionalization or keeping the individual at home with no services. Now there are a number of vocational-training centers for adults and developmental day-care centers for children who are excluded from public schools due to age or multiple handicapping conditions. In addition to these developmental centers, several regional offices are using generic early-education and preschool programs to serve the mentally retarded preschool population. The state has also developed adult training residences, staffed apartments, independent-living apartments, children's and adolescents' group homes, foster homes, behavior-shaping units and other types of residential options.[1]

If the state denies a person his liberty or otherwise accepts responsibility for him because he is mentally retarded, the due process clause and the Eighth Amendment require that this custody must serve the purpose of his habilitation with the ultimate aim of enhancing his ability to function autonomously in the community and of restoring his liberty. (See pp. 57-73 below.) Mental-retardation experts agree that the most effective approach to maximizing a mentally retarded person's functioning capacity involves imposing no more restrictions than are absolutely necessary—and this in turn requires access to a continuum of different kinds of habilitation facilities suited to individual needs.

Do mentally retarded persons have a right to be habilitated in settings less restrictive than institutions where feasible?

Yes. The right to habilitation in the least restrictive setting necessary to accomplish legitimate habilitation goals would appear to be a constitutional requirement as well as a sound habilitation principle. In keeping with the Supreme Court's holding that "even though the governmental purpose be legitimate and substantial, that purpose cannot be pursued by means that broadly stifle fundamental personal liberties when the end can be more narrowly achieved," [2] three recent Federal-court decisions have held that prior to involuntary hospitalization of the mentally handicapped, the Constitution requires a demonstration that there are no appropriate less restrictive alternatives.[3] The order entered by the district court in another recent decision specifically bans commitment to an institution "unless 'a prior determination shall have been made that residence in the institution is the least restrictive habilitation setting feasible for that person." [4]

Moreover, several states explicitly authorize or compel their courts to use less restrictive alternatives in commitment cases.[5] And even where state statutes do not expressly provide for less restrictive alternatives, the right to be habilitated in a less restrictive setting may be inferred from right-to-habilitation language in the state statute or legislative history. In a landmark case in the District of Columbia, individual plaintiffs confined to Saint Elizabeths Hospital sued on their own behalf and on behalf of other persons similarly situated for a declaration that under the District's Hospitalization of the Mentally Ill Act, they had a right to placement in facilities outside Saint Elizabeths Hospital, where such placement would be consistent with the habilitative purposes of the Act. Alternative facilities were defined as including but not limited to nursing homes, personal-care homes, foster homes and halfway houses. In the estimation of the hospital's clinical staff, approximately 43 percent of the inpatients at Saint Elizabeths Hospital (including mentally retarded persons) currently required care and treatment in alternative facilities. But these residents were forced to remain at Saint Elizabeths Hospital because adequate community facilities did not exist. On December 23, 1975, a Federal district court held that residents of Saint Elizabeths did have the right to be treated in appropriate less restrictive facilities. The court held further that the District of Columbia and Federal governments had a joint responsibility to initiate a plan for development of alternative facilities and the placement of apropriate individuals therein.[6]

A mentally retarded person who voluntarily seeks habilitation is free to make his own selection of facility. However, in states which lack community habilitation programs, sheltered workshops and neighborhood social-service units, this principle of providing habilitation in the least restrictive setting cannot be meaningfully applied. Often the only realistic choices are between total institutionalization at a state hospital or training school and no services at all.

The right to be habilitated in the least restrictive facility is based not only on habilitation theory and on constitutional law, but also on Federal statutory law. The Developmentally Disabled Assistance and Bill of Rights Act, passed in 1975, specifically states that "the treatment, services, and habilitation for a person with developmental disabilities . . . should be provided in the setting that is least restrictive of the person's personal liberty." [7] State legislatures, too, are beginning to recognize this important right.[8] The excuse that a state lacks financial resources to construct and implement habilitation services is not a sufficient response to the problem. (See discussion at pp. 64-65 below.)

By what means are mentally retarded persons admitted to public institutions?

Admission to public habilitation facilities is either through voluntary application or involuntary commitment. When a mentally retarded person "voluntarily" seeks admission to a facility, some states inquire whether he is competent to do so—that is, whether he understands the nature and consequences of his application. If a facility or court finds that the applicant lacks the capacity to understand the meaning of his "voluntary" application, the school or court may require a hearing to determine whether institutionalization is in the applicant's best interest.

"Voluntary" admissions approved by a parent or

guardian in the name of a mentally retarded person are frequently permitted and are probably the most common way by which mentally retarded persons find their way into institutions. (See pp. 36-38 below.) They are not sufficient unless accompanied by proof that the person is incompetent to make his own decision about admission and that institutionalization is the most appropriate form of habilitation. Unfortunately, few states require this showing. A related form of "voluntary" application involves the application by parents on behalf of their minor children. Because of potential conflicts of interest between parents and their mentally retarded offspring, "voluntary" commitment of a mentally retarded child by his parent(s) should be subject to review. (See pp. 36-38 below.)

Involuntary commitment procedures can be initiated by a variety of persons for a variety of reasons. Petitions for commitment are commonly filed by friends, relatives or "interested persons," or initiated by a court or public-health agency. Upon filing of the petition and supporting certificate required to substantiate the subject's mental condition, a judicial or administrative inquiry is held into the mental condition of the subject and his need for care and habilitation. These commitment hearings result either in dismissal of the commitment petition or in commitment.

Some states—for example, Massachusetts—have abolished all commitments to institutions for the mentally retarded; only so-called "voluntary" admissions are possible.[9]

What are the grounds for involuntary commitment of mentally retarded persons?

In order to be committed involuntarily in some states, the mentally retarded person must be dangerous to himself or others by reason of his mental condition.[10] Other states allow confinement of a mentally retarded person on the ground that he is in need of care and treatment.[11] Still other states allow commitment on the basis of mental retardation alone, without any requirement either of dangerousness or of need for care.[12] But these standards are vague and overbroad. Even if they are narrowed by inclusion of a dangerousness requirement, predictions of future dangerous behavior are notoriously inaccurate.[13] Therefore, many experts agree that involuntary commitment should be allowed only after objective proof of the presence of mental retardation *and* upon the basis of demonstrated past action which indicates substantial incapacity on the part of the mentally retarded person to prevent harm to himself or to other people. Other constitutional limitations on involuntary commitment of mentally retarded persons are discussed under the question which follows.

What procedures and standards are required for involuntary commitment of mentally retarded persons?

Since involuntary commitment to any facility involves a deprivation of liberty and other related rights and privileges, it cannot be legally imposed without certain procedural safeguards. In *Dixon* v. *Attorney General*,[14] a Federal court in Pennsylvania detailed some of the constitutional requirements for involuntary commitment procedures affecting mentally retarded persons. According to the *Dixon* court, the mentally retarded person subject to commitment is entitled to notice and a hearing on the issue of commitment, the assistance of counsel and a mental examination by an independent expert to be appointed by the court if the person is indigent. There must be a full hearing at which the allegedly mentally retarded person "shall have the right to present evidence in his own behalf, to subpoena witnesses and documents, and to confront and cross-examine all witnesses against him." [15] A person may be committed only if unequivocal and convincing evidence establishes that he "poses a present threat of serious physical harm to other persons or to himself." [16]

While some courts require dangerousness to be proved "beyond a reasonable doubt," most jurisdictions allow commitment on the basis of "clear and convincing evidence." Commitments must also be limited to a definite period of time. At the expiration of this term, if continued confinement is still thought to be desirable, a new commitment proceeding must be instituted.

As discussed at p. 30 above, placement must be in the least restrictive alternative setting consistent with effective habilitation for the particular person involved. Experts also have suggested and courts have required that an individual habilitation plan should be established *before* final placement pursuant to commitment is ordered. Throughout the course of commitment, the person's mental and physical condition must be reviewed periodically to assure the appropriateness of the current habilitation plan and physical conditions of confinement.

Taken together, these requirements establish minimally adequate commitment procedures. Unfortunately, many current state laws fall short of providing these procedures and standards. Some state codes are entirely silent on commitment procedures for mentally retarded persons, while others explicitly apply the inappropriate rules used in the commitment of mentally ill persons. The absence of strict standards and procedures prior to the deprivation of liberty through commitment cannot be justified by benign motives or the fact that the "civil" commitment does not involve punishment for a crime. As noted by a Federal court of appeals which considered appropriate standards for the commitment of mentally retarded juveniles,

"It matters not whether the proceedings be labeled 'civil' or 'criminal' or whether the subject matter be mental instability or juvenile delinquency. It is the likelihood of involuntary incarceration—whether for punishment as an adult for a crime, rehabilitation as a juvenile for delinquency, or treatment and training as a feeble-minded or mental incompetent—which commands observance of the constitutional safeguards of due process. Where, as in both proceedings for juveniles and mentally deficient persons, the state undertakes to act in parens patriae, it has the inescapable duty to vouchsafe due process. . . ." [17]

Do separate legal issues or procedures apply to the commitment of mentally retarded children?

There are no laws which establish a comprehensive set of separate procedures for the commitment of children. Too commonly, the result is that laws governing adult commitment are improperly applied to juveniles or adapted piecemeal through administrative discretion, which is sometimes well-intentioned but frequently uninformed. As one commentator has noted sadly, "The current juvenile commitment system contains no due process protections. No notice, no hearing, no counsel, no cross-examination, no witnesses are required. No burden or standard of proof exists because nothing need be proven." [18]

One of the most serious abuses of due process is the relatively widespread practice of "voluntary" commitment of children to facilities for the mentally retarded on the unreviewed application of their parents. (Under many statutes, parental consent is also required before mentally retarded children can be discharged from habilitation facilities.) Courts have only recently begun to enforce constitutional protections for juveniles subject to such deprivations of liberty. [19] Tennessee, Pennsylvania and Georgia no longer give parents unreviewed discretion to control the commitment and release of their minor children. Recent court decisions in these three states recognize that, contrary to the usual assumptions about parental motives, there may be a serious conflict of interest between juveniles and parents who seek to confine them.[20] As noted by the court in *Bartley v. Kremens,* "In deciding to institutionalize their children, parents, as well as guardians . . . may at times be acting against the interest of their children." [21] Strong pressures lead parents to institutionalize mentally retarded children: The financial demands upon a family with a mentally retarded child, the tremendous difficulty of securing the varied resources required to care for a severely, multiply handicapped child at home, the social and/or psychological pressures on parents to avoid the guilt and stigma frequently associated with having a mentally retarded child. These factors make necessary the intervention of a neutral party to determine whether the child's commitment can in fact be justified by institutionalized-habilitation possibilities or whether commitment is only in the parents' interests. The *Bartley* court ruled that "in the absence of evidence that the child's interests have been fully considered, parents may not effectively waive personal constitutional rights of their children." [22]

The potentially coercive effect of "voluntary" admissions by parents and guardians is also recognized by newly enacted commitment legislation in Ohio.[23] Under previous law, a parent or guardian could "voluntarily" admit a mentally retarded individual to a state institution. Persons who had provided their own volition for their admission had a right to release or hearing upon request, yet where the parent or guardian had provided the volition, the right to release could be conditioned upon the consent of that parent. The new statute provides that the mentally retarded individual always has the right to release upon request, unless the managing officer of the institution files a petiton for involuntary admission within three court days.

Thus, the "voluntary" admission process is purified: active opposition to continued institutionalization negates voluntary status.

If anything, a child's inherently limited ability to defend his own interests argues for even stricter protections in the commitment process than adults should enjoy. According to the *Bartley* court, mentally retarded children may not be civilly committed without the following minimum constitutional safeguards: (1) a probable-cause hearing within 72 hours of the child's initial detention; (2) a post-commitment hearing to be held not more than two weeks after initial detention; (3) written notice, including the date, time and place of the commitment hearing and a statement of grounds for the proposed commitment; (4) counsel at all significant stages of the commitment process (to be appointed by the court if the child is indigent); (5) presence of the child at all hearings concerning his proposed commitment; (6) a finding by clear and convincing proof that the child is in need of institutionalization; and (7) the right of the child and his lawyer to confront and cross-examine witnesses against him, to offer evidence in his own behalf and to offer testimony of witnesses.[24]

How does admission to a habilitation facility affect the legal rights of mentally retarded persons?

Some states automatically impose certain legal or civil disabilities on mentally retarded persons who have been committed, such as the loss of the right to vote or to marry. But the provision of habilitation services is not a sufficient reason for limiting a recipient's legal rights. The better approach is shown by state statutes which explicitly provide that "no person shall be deprived of any civil right, or public or private employment, solely by reason of his having received services, voluntarily or involuntarily, for mental retardation."[25] Particular legal disabilities should be imposed only after satisfactory procedural safeguards have been observed.

What are the grounds for release from a habilitation facility?

An involuntarily confined mentally retarded person is entitled to be discharged if, due either to his successful habilitation or to the absence of effective services, the particular placement is no longer appropriate. Obviously, where the justification for commitment is habilitation and where effective habilitation is not in fact delivered, the person committed is entitled to release.[26]

Closely related is the right of institutionalized mentally retarded persons to periodic review of their progress and of the continuing necessity for their placement.[27] If habilitation is effective it will result in the individual's enhanced functioning ability. A higher level of actual competence may well call for re-evaluation of the current placement with an eye toward providing accelerated or more advanced services in less restrictive and more "normal" settings. A person voluntarily admitted to a habilitation facility should, of course, be entitled to release whenever he asks to be released.

NOTES

1. Glenn, "The Least Restrictive Alternative in Residential Care and the Principle of Normalization," in *The Mentally Retarded Citizen and the Law* (M. Kindred et al., eds. 1976); *See also* Neb. Rev. Stat. §§83-1,142 to 1,144.01 (Cum. Supp. 1974).
2. *Shelton v. Tucker*, 364 U.S. 479, 488 (1960) (footnote omitted).
3. *Covington v. Harris*, 419 F.2d 616, 623 (D.C. Cir. 1969); *Lessard v. Schmidt*, 349 F. Supp. 1078, 1095-97 (E.D. Wis. 1972), *vacated for entry of more*

specific relief, 414 U.S. 473 (1974), *on remand*, 379 F.Supp. 1376 (E.D. Wis. 1974), *vacated on other grounds*, 421 U.S. 957 (1975), *redecided*—F. Supp. —(E.D. Wis. 1976); *Dixon v. Attorney General*, 325 F.Supp. 966, 974 (M.D. Pa. 1971).

4. *Wyatt v. Stickney*, 344 F. Supp. 387, 396 (M.D. Ala. 1972), *aff'd in part, remanded in part sub nom. Wyatt v. Aderholt*, 503 F.2d 1305 (5th Cir. 1974) (footnote omitted).

5. *See, e.g.*, New Mexico Stat. Ann. §34-3-6 (mental defectives who are assured of adequate care and supervision and who are not a public menace are excluded from the involuntary commitment provisions); §34-2-5 (commitment of mentally ill requires consideration of less restrictive alternatives) (Supp. 1975).

6. *Dixon v. Weinberger*, 405 F.Supp. 974 (D.D.C. 1975).

7. Pub. L. No. 94-103, 89 Stat. 486, §201 (Oct. 4, 1975), *to be codified at* 42 U.S.C. §6010. *See also id.* §§110(b), 111(a), *to be codified at* 42 U.S.C. §§6062-63 (states required to eliminate inappropriate placements in institutions).

8. "In determining the place to which or the person with whom the [retarded person] is to be committed, the court shall consider the comprehensive evaluation, diagnosis, and projected habilitation plan . . . and order the implementation of the least restrictive alternative available and consistent with habilitation goals." Ohio Rev. Code Ann. §5123.76(E) (Page Supp. 1974).

* * *

"If at any time it is determined by the director of the facility or the program to which or the person to whom the [retarded person] is committed that [such person] could be equally well habilitated in a less restrictive environment which is available:

(1) [such person] shall be released [from the current facility] forthwith and referred to the court. . . .

* * *

(3) The court shall dismiss the case or order placement in the less restrictive environment. *Id.*§5123.76(F).

9. Mass. Gen. Laws Ann. ch. 123, §§ 1 *et seq.* (1972), *as amended*, (Supp. 1974). Dr. Gunnar Dybwad, Gingold Professor of Human Development, Florence Heller Graduate School for Advanced Studies in Social Welfare, Brandeis University, has observed to the author in a letter dated November 18, 1975, that the Massachusetts approach has worked quite successfully.

10. *E.g.*, Wash. Rev. Code Ann. §71.05.040(1975), *as amended*, ch. 199, §1 [June 16, 1975] Wash. Laws, 1st Ex. Sess., *reported at* 2 Wash. Leg. Serv. 585 (1975).

11. For example, a person in Utah can be involuntarily committed if he is "so mentally retarded as to be unable to properly care for himself." Utah Code Ann. §64-8-20 (Supp. 1975).

12. *See, e.g.*, Conn. Gen. Stat. Ann. §17-172d (1975). Pub. Act No. 75-5 (Mar. 25, 1975), *reported at* 1 Conn. Leg. Serv. 5 (1975), deleted the two-year residency requirement and the inclusion of epileptics within the section.

13. *See, e.g.*, Ennis & Litwack, "Psychiatry and the Presumption of Expertise: Flipping Coins in the Courtroom," 62 *Calif. L. Rev.* 693 (1974).

14. *Dixon v. Attorney General*, 325 F.Supp. 966 (M.D. Pa. 1971).

15. *Id.* at 974.

16. *Id.*

17. *Heryford v. Parker*, 396 F.2d 393, 396 (10th Cir. 1968).

18. Ellis, "Volunteering Children: Parental Commitment of Minors to Mental Institutions," 62 *Calif. L. Rev.* 841, 901 (1974).

19. State courts in Connecticut and Illinois have held that such ostensibly voluntary commitments of their children by parents or guardians violate due process and have ordered competent juveniles age 16 and above to be released upon their own request regardless of parental consent. *Melville v. Sabbatino, re-*

ported in part at 42 U.S.L.W. 2242 (Oct. 5, 1973); *In re Lee,* No. 68 (JD) 1362 (Cook County, Ill. Cir. Ct., Aug. 24, 1972), *abstr'd in* 6 Clearinghouse Review 575 (Jan. 1973).

20. *Saville v. Treadway,* Civil Action No. Nashville 6969 (M.D. Tenn., Mar. 8, 1974), *consent decree entered,* Sept. 18, 1974; *Bartley v. Kremens,* 402 F.Supp. 1039, 1047-48 (E.D. Pa.), *stay granted,* 96 S.Ct. 558, *probable jurisdiction noted,* 96 S.Ct. 1457 (March 22, 1976); *J.L. v. Parham,* —F.Supp. —, No. 75-163 M.A.C. (M.D. Ga. 1976), *stay granted,* 96 S.Ct.1503(1976).

21. 402 F. Supp. at 1047-48.

22. *Id.* at 1048.

23. Ohio Rev. Code Ann. §§5123.67 *et. seq.* (Page Supp. 1974). §5123.70 in particular explicitly provides for the release upon request of one voluntarily admitted.

24. 402 F. Supp. at 1053.

25. Ohio Rev. Code Ann. §5123.83 (Page Supp. 1974).

26. *See* discussion of *O'Connor v. Donaldson* at pp. 91-93 below.

27. *See* Mass. Gen. Laws Ann. ch. 123, §4 (Supp. 1974); Mich. Stat. Ann. §14.800(531) (Supp. 1975).

RIGHTS IN COMPETENCY AND GUARDIANSHIP PROCEEDINGS

Aren't all mentally retarded persons legally incompetent?

No. In most states, a mentally retarded person is legally incompetent only if there is a court order or administrative determination to that effect. Although the laws of some states allow an inference of incompetence on the basis of civil commitment proceedings, these automatic inferences do not satisfy the requirements of due process.

Are mentally retarded persons either competent for all purposes or competent for none?

No. In the past, the concept of incompetence was applied in a clumsy, all-or-nothing way. But applied properly, it relates to qualifications for specific activities.[1] A person may be competent to perform some acts but not others—for example, incapable of managing complicated financial affairs but able to handle personal matters perfectly well. The law should recognize this person's competence in the latter area and treat him only as financially incompetent.

Item-specific incompetence is now recognized in a growing number of states.[2] In these states, the acts of a mentally retarded person are legally recognized in the same manner as are the acts of a normal person, except when a mentally retarded person has been declared incompetent to perform a particular action. Hence, in states like Minnesota and Michigan, which recognize these distinctions, the retarded person who is legally incompetent to make a binding business contract may nevertheless be legally competent to marry. Unhappily, not all states have such enlightened laws. Many continue to make blanket determinations of incompetence which apply to all activities.

Should mentally retarded persons admitted to institutions be presumed legally incompetent?

No. Admission of a mentally retarded person to a habilitation facility should not be interpreted to mean that he is legally incompetent. Whether a person should be committed to an institution and whether he is legally incompetent are separate questions and their answers involve separate considerations. It cannot be presumed that all persons who may benefit from habilitation are in need of someone to handle their affairs for them. When a mentally retarded person's institutional residence is a product of his voluntary application rather than his involuntary commitment, there is little basis indeed for a presumption of incompetence.

Nevertheless, some states do still take the unsound position that entry to an institution establishes legal incompetence. And a number of states allow treatment facilities to make administrative determinations about a resident's legal competence or to restrict his civil rights, even though admission to the facility alone does not establish legal incompetence. The more progressive position is taken by states which explicitly provide that institutionalization does not terminate or limit a person's legal rights in the absence of a separate express determination of legal incompetence.[3] Administrative policies which restrict a person's basic civil rights or his access to the normal privileges of citizenship, absent a specific finding of his legal incompetence to exercise them, violate due process. Some states have a "bill of rights" for mentally retarded persons resident in treatment facilities in order expressly to guarantee the continued vitality of their rights.[4]

What is a guardian?

A guardian is a person who has legal authority to make certain decisions on behalf of and in the best interest of another person who is unable to make those decisions himself.

When is a guardian appointed for a mentally retarded person?

Generally, a guardian is appointed when a mentally retarded person is determined to be legally incompetent to manage certain aspects of his own affairs.

How does the principle of the least restrictive alternative apply in the area of guardianship?

Two important and valid policy goals are in tension in the guardianship area. The first goal is to protect mentally retarded persons from exploitation; the second goal is to maximize the freedom of mentally retarded persons and their opportunities to function with autonomy in the community. In most situations these goals can be reconciled so as to provide necessary protections without imposing unnecessary restrictions on personal autonomy. The legal principle of the least restrictive alternative governs such attempts to reconcile conflicts between the individual's constitutionally protected interest in his freedom and autonomy and the state's interest in acting like a good parent. As discussed at pp. 30-32 above, this principle requires that even where the government has a compelling public goal which justifies intrusion upon an individual's more personal interest, the overriding public interests must be precisely defined and the intrusion must be no more than is absolutely necessary for their accomplishment.

Application of this principle in the guardianship area has led to creation both of specialized forms of guardians which are less restrictive alternatives to the old total-guardianship concept and to some important less restrictive alternatives to guardianship itself. On a continuum, guardianship can be viewed as a less restrictive alternative to institutionalization, and certain supportive social services can be viewed in turn as less restrictive alternatives to guardianship.

What are the different forms of guardianship for mentally retarded persons?

The form and extent of guardianship should depend on the needs of the person for whom the guardian is appointed. General guardianship is the broadest and most comprehensive instrument for control. It transfers total transactional power to the guardian as substitute decision-maker. While some mentally retarded persons may be so incapable of any independent decision-making that general guardianship will be required, such a complete abdication of self-control will over-restrict the great majority of mentally retarded persons, stifling the potential for independent living. An International Symposium on Guardianship recently concluded that: "The ability to assert one's rights or express one's wishes is seldom completely lacking. The retarded adult should be permitted to act for himself in those matters in which he has competence. The limitations of legal capacity inherent in guardianship should not extend to these matters. It follows that a person whose mental retardation is characterized by impairments of social competence which are partial should enjoy a partial guardianship specifically adapted to his strengths and weaknesses." [5] Recognizing this principle, many states have created different forms of guardianship and provide separately for the appointment of "guardians of the estate" (or "conservators"), "guardians for the person" and guardians *ad litem.*

Guardianship of the estate allows and requires the guardian to replace his ward in transactions dealing with the management of property and income. Guardianship of the person gives the guardian custody over the ward, with the right to determine where and how he should live and with responsibility for education, training and personal welfare. Guardians *ad litem* are appointed for the specific purpose of conducting litigation on behalf of their wards. In most states the same person can be appointed guardian of these separate interests.

As an extension of the principle of least restrictive alternative, one expert has suggested development of "facilitative guardianships" as alternatives to control guardianships.[6] The "facilitator guardian" would have no power to substitute his own power for that of the ward but would retain responsibility for supporting the ward in major decisions involving the use of his contractual power.

How do supportive social services—such as the provision of an advocate or a protector—provide a less restrictive alternative to guardianship?

Guardianship is sometimes described as a social service. But guardianship's essential characteristic is that it removes choices from the mentally retarded individual (giving them to the guardian), whereas social services in the community expand choices.[7] Experts argue that neither institutionalization nor guardianship are necessary for most mentally retarded persons if there are adequate supportive social services to expand the range of choices in areas like housing, employment and education, along with adequate personal-support services in such areas as homemaking and money management.

Two specialized personal services deserve attention. The first is that of an advocate.[8] The role of the advocate is both to create pressure for better social-service programs for his client and to help his client to locate and secure access to existing services. While a guardian can, of course, play such an advocacy role, advocacy does not require or depend upon the control that typifies a guardianship.

Another service role is that of a "ombudsman" or "protector." The role of the protector is to monitor guardians and to provide a countercheck. Under Ohio law, for example, a "protector" acts

> "with or without court appointment to provide guidance, service, and encouragement in the development of maximum self-reliance to a mentally retarded or other developmentally disabled person, independent of any determination of incompetency." [9]

Another very specific protective role is relegated to the Ohio Division of Mental Retardation by a recently enacted requirement that professionals report any incident of suspected abuse or neglect of a mentally retarded adult to the division for investigation.[10]

Under New York law, the New York Mental Health Information Service is charged with the protective duties of informing residents and interested parties of residents' rights and of providing service and assistance to residents and their families.[11]

How are trusts used to safeguard the future of mentally retarded children?

Trusts are another existing legal mechanism which can be used to provide a limited degree of control and protection without the massive restrictions of general guardianship. Trusts can serve as instruments by which parents and relatives convey significant property to mentally retarded beneficiaries, subject to certain control. Living trusts are trusts created during the lifetime of the parent or relative ("settlor") and are revocable and amendable. Testamentary trusts are trusts created by will, to take effect upon the death of the settlor. Conceptually, trusts are based upon the principle that persons may dispose of their property upon such reasonable conditions as they choose. A mentally retarded person who is the beneficiary of a trust remains free to make the same choices he could make in the absence of the trust. He is simply presented with additional choices that may be required if he wishes to enjoy the trust proceeds.

One expert has described the advantages of a trust as follows:

"(1) It provides management of funds and property to see that maximum income consistent with safety of principal is produced;

(2) it can provide a mechanism for expenditure of funds, with the trustee paying bills, contracting for care and, as appropriate, paying modest amounts of cash directly to the re-

tarded beneficiary. In some cases this may eliminate the need for a guardian. The trustee can perform most of the functions a guardian would;

(3) the trust can provide maximum flexibility in use of both principal and income by resting broad powers and discretion in the trustee, such as a power to accumulate income when not needed and to invade principal when income is inadequate for current needs;

(4) the trust can be adapted to the individual situation in light of the assets, the needs of other members of the family, and the desires of the parents;

(5) on termination of the trust, the remaining funds can be distributed to other family members without death taxes or probate expense." [12]

How is a guardian appointed?

A guardian is usually appointed by a court in a guardianship proceeding. But a judicial proceeding may not occur in states which allow hospital directors or public officials to act as guardians, or where a guardianship is created by will upon the death of the retarded person's parents (his "natural" guardians).

A court may consider the appointment of a guardian on the basis of a request or "petition" which can be submitted by a variety of individuals. Some states will only honor the request of a member of the person's family or circle of friends, while courts in other jurisdictions will determine incompetence and appoint a guardian on the application of any "interested person" or designated public official. Some courts initiate incompetence or guardianship proceedings on their own. These "ex parte" proceedings do not require anyone to file a petition with the court, but still require a final judicial order.

Since appointment of a guardian can operate to deny a person the right to act on his own behalf in matters of fundamental interest,[13] guardianship proceedings should involve adequate procedural safeguards to make sure that the prospective ward's interests are fully represented. At a minimum the prospective ward should be notified that a guardianship is being contemplated, that he has the right to appear at the proceedings and contest the appointment through his own testimony and the appearance of sympathetic witnesses, and that he will receive the assistance of counsel who has the duty to assure full exploration of considerations against imposition of guardianship.[14] There must be a presumption against general guardianship and in favor of less restrictive alternatives to guardianship, and the appointment of a guardian must be subject to periodic review. The extent to which these due process requirements are actually observed varies from state to state.

What effect does legal incompetence or appointment of a guardian have on a mentally retarded person's property transactions?

In many states, legal incompetence or the appointment of a guardian interferes with the legal effect given to a mentally retarded person's property transactions. Contracts for sales and services will not be binding if one of the parties to them is legally incompetent. If a person acquires "title" or legal ownership of property whose former owner was mentally retarded, the passage of title from the mentally retarded owner may not be legally valid unless it was explicitly approved by his guardian. The absence of a guardian's approval for a property transaction by a legally incompetent metally retarded person is considered a "cloud" on the title to the property.

Some title insurance companies will not insure the "good title" of property formerly owned by a legally incompetent mentally retarded person. Also the rights of current property owners may be vulnerable to legal attack if they are based on a passage or chain of title which includes an incompetent title holder. As the preceding discussion should have established, a previous owner's mental retardation by itself should not justify failure to insure his title, nor should it lead to questioning of the property rights of successor owners unless the previous owner was legally incompetent at the time he executed the transaction.

How does a person regain his legal competence?

A person's legal competence is restored when the law recognizes that he is capable of handling his own affairs. When incompetence has been formally established by court order, an independent proceeding to restore competence and a judicial order must be obtained. Various persons are authorized to submit petitions to restore competence to an incompetent person. In some states, if a person has been pronounced incompetent to conduct legal proceedings, he can initiate a petition for the restoration of his own competence only through his guardian *ad litem*. Where incompetence is automatically established by institutionalization, release from the institution frequently operates to restore competence. But a person's actual incompetence to perform certain tasks can survive his release from an institution. Automatic and complete restoration upon discharge is just as unfounded as is automatic and complete denial of competence upon admission.

Are there any ways to review the guardian's management of his ward's property?

Yes. A guardian must exercise great care in managing his ward's property.[15] This obligation is sometimes termed a "fiduciary duty" which attaches to any relationship in which the law will imply a foundation of trust. A guardian is entrusted with his ward's assets and must exercise his authority in the best interests of the ward. Typically, state laws prohibit a guardian from wasting his ward's assets and require the guardian to apply them only in the ward's interest and for his benefit. Some states require a candidate for appointment as guardian to post a money bond which may be forfeited for breach of duty and which may be used to satisfy money judgments against the guardian for mismanagement. Also, some states mandate periodic accounting or will order a guardian to give a financial report of the ward's estate on the petition of the ward, his relatives or interested parties.

Should officials of public agencies or habilitation facilities be allowed to act as financial guardians of mentally retarded residents?

No. Laws which allow the officials of public health departments or treatment facilities to act as financial guardians for mentally retarded residents of the facilities should be challenged because they create serious conflicts of interest and possibilities for mismanagement. Such appointments make the state the payor for the same person billed for services. The potential conflict of interest in an institution's position as creditor and guardian are apparent. Such a conflict is not only unfair to the financial interests of the mentally retarded ward but also compromises the position of other creditors.

For these reasons, a Federal district court recently ruled unconstitutional a Connecticut statute which provided for the appointment of the state Commissioner of Finance as conservator for the funds of residents of mental institutions whose assets totaled less than $5,000. The court ruled that this procedure violated petitioner's right to due process of law because the conservator was appointed without any hearing to determine that the resident was incompetent to manage his own financial affairs. The provision also violated the equal protection clause because other statutes required notice and hearing before a conservator could be appointed for more affluent or noninstitutionalized persons.[16]

How and under what conditions can a guardianship be challenged and terminated?

A guardianship can be terminated if the guardian abuses his authority or if his services are no longer needed.

Termination of guardianship because of the ward's recovery of competence can be sought by a variety of persons. Where competence has been legally restored to the ward in a separate proceeding, he may himself seek the guardian's discharge. When his legal competence has never been denied and the guardian or advocate has functioned supportively but not as a legal surrogate, the guardian's tasks and authority should be regularly reviewed and altered if necessary to comply with the ward's legal needs. Typical statutory provisions are phrased to permit termination or change of the guardian's duty and authority upon the petition of a guardian himself, his ward or another interested person.

NOTES

1. *See* International League of Societies for the Mentally Handicapped, *Symposium on Guardianship of the Mentally Retarded* 18-19 (1969) (hereinafter "Symposium"). For an excellent exploration of guardianship problems *see generally* Kindred, "Guardianship and Limitations upon Capacity," in *The Mentally Retarded Citizen and the Law* (M. Kindred et al., eds. 1976) (hereinafter "Kindred").
2. *E.g.*, Mich. Stat. Ann. §14.800(620) (Supp. 1975); Ch. 208, §11 [June 2, 1975] Minn. Laws, 1st Reg.

Sess., *to be codified at* Minn. Stat. Ann. §252 A.11, *reported in* 4 Minn. Sess. Law Serv. 520 (1975).

3. *See* N.D. Cent. Code §25-03-20 (Replacement Vol. 4 1970); N.Y. Mental Hygiene Law §15.01 (McKinney Supp. 1975-76). However, some states, like Texas, merely require a district-court finding on the issue of competence as part of the commitment hearing. Tex. Rev. Civ. Stat. Ann. art. 5547-51(1958).

4. *See., e.g.,* The Bill of Rights of Retarded Persons, Fla. Stat. Ann. §393.13 (Supp. 1975).

5. Symposium, *supra,* note 1, at 18-19.

6. Kindred, *supra,* note 1.

7. *Id.*

8. W. Wolfensberger, *Toward Citizen Advocacy for the Handicapped, Impaired, and Disadvantaged* (rev. ed. 1971).

9. Ohio Rev. Code Ann. §5119.85(D) (Page Supp. 1974). A possible conflict-of-interest problem arises since the protector under this statute is the Division of Mental Retardation or an agency under contract with it.

10. *Id.* §5123.98.

11. N.Y. Mental Hygiene Law §29.09 (McKinney Supp. 1975-76).

12. Effland, "Trusts and Estate Planning," in *The Mentally Retarded Citizen and the Law* (M. Kindred et al., eds. 1976).

13. In many states, guardians are authorized to execute "voluntary" applications for admission to habilitation facilities and mental hospitals [Ga. Code Ann. §88-2503 (1971)] and to initiate "voluntary" sterilization proceedings on behalf of their wards [Vt. Stat. Ann. tit. 18, §8702(C)(1968)]. Recently, statutes authorizing guardians to execute pseudo-voluntary applications for admission in the name of their minor wards have been declared unconstitutional. *See Saville v. Treadway,* Civil Action No. Nashville 6969 (M.D. Tenn., Mar. 8, 1974), *consent decree entered,* Sept. 18, 1974; *Bartley v. Kremens,* 402 F. Supp. 1039 1047-48 (E.D. Pa. 1975), *stay granted,* 96 S.Ct. 558, *probable jurisdiction noted,* 96 S.Ct. 1457 (March 22, 1976); *J. L. v. Parham,*—F.Supp.—, No. 75-163

M.A.C. (M.D. Ga. 1976), *stay granted*, 96 S.Ct. 1503 (1976).

14. New York is among the states which require notice, judicial hearings and assistance of counsel prior to the appointment of financial or personal guardians. N.Y. Mental Hygiene Law §§77.07, 78.03 (McKinney Supp. 1975-76).

15. The precise standard of care to which guardians are held varies from state to state.

16. *McAuliffe v. Carlson*, 377 F. Supp. 896 (D. Conn. 1974). A supplemental decision, 386 F. Supp. 1245, was reversed on other grounds, 520 F.2d 1305 (2d Cir. 1975).

III

Rights of Mentally Retarded Persons in Institutions

THE RIGHT TO HABILITATION AND THE RIGHT TO PROTECTION FROM HARM

Do civilly committed mentally retarded persons have a right to habilitation? [1]

Yes. Some states' statutes expressly provide that persons committed to state institutions for the mentally retarded have a right to habilitation. [2]

Even more important, however, is the growing recognition that even in those states where the legislatures have not acted to recognize a right to habilitation, such a right may be guaranteed by the United States Constitution. On April 13, 1972, a United States District Court in *Wyatt v. Stickney* [3] made history by ruling for the first time that mentally retarded persons involuntarily confined to a state institution had a constitutional right to habilitation.

In an equally historic decision, the Fifth Circuit Court of Appeals became the first U.S. appellate court to affirm the constitutional right to habilitation for the mentally retarded. The Court of Appeals based its decision in *Wyatt* upon its earlier decision in the related case, *Donaldson v. O'Connor,* [4] in which a former mental patient was awarded damages against a superintendent and one of his treating psychiatrists because he had been confined for fifteen years without treatment, his efforts to be released consistently blocked by the defendants.

Since *Wyatt,* similar results have been obtained in Nebraska,[5] Minnesota,[6] Massachusetts[7] and Tennessee.[8] Additional litigation designed to establish that mentally retarded persons have a constitutional right to habilitation is under way in the District of Columbia, California, Georgia, Maine, Maryland, Mississippi, Missouri, Montana, Ohio, Pennsylvania and Washington.

What are mentally retarded persons entitled to under a constitutional right to habilitation?

The *Wyatt* court found that the three essential elements of meaningful habilitation were a humane psychological and physical environment, an individualized habilitation and training plan for each resident and qualified professional and paraprofessional staff in sufficient numbers to deliver individualized habilitation and training. More specifically, the standards which the *Wyatt* court ordered the state of Alabama to implement included prohibition against institutional peonage; a number of protections to insure a humane psychological environment; minimum staffing ratios; detailed physical standards; minimum nutritional requirements; individualized evaluations of residents, habilitation plans and programs; a requirement that residents released from Partlow State School would be provided with appropriate transitional care; and a requirement that every mentally retarded person has a right to the least restrictive setting necessary for habilitation.

The *Wyatt* court also appointed a seven-member "human rights committee" for Partlow State School and included a mentally retarded resident on this committee. The human rights committee "review[s] . . . all research proposals and all habilitation programs to ensure that the dignity and human rights of residents are preserved." It also advises and assists residents who allege that their legal rights have been infringed or that the mental-health board has failed to comply with the judicially ordered guidelines.

These standards were agreed upon and recommended to the court by plaintiffs, defendants, the United States Department of Health, Education and Welfare and a number of mental-health and retardation professional and consumer organizations which had participated as *amici curiae* (friends of the court) in the *Wyatt* litigation. They were supported in written and oral testimony by nationally recognized experts who participated in the *Wyatt* proceedings.

What were the conditions addressed by the Wyatt Right-to-Habilitation litigation?

After taking evidence during a hearing on the need for emergency relief to "protect the lives and well-being of the residents of Partlow," the *Wyatt* court found that:

"The evidence . . . has vividly and undisputedly portrayed Partlow State School and Hospital as a warehousing institution which, because of its atmosphere of psychological and physical deprivation, is wholly incapable of furnishing habilitation to the mentally retarded and is conducive only to the deterioration and the debilitation of the residents. The evidence has reflected further that safety and sanitary conditions at Partlow are substandard to the point of endangering the health and lives of those residing there, that the wards are grossly understaffed, rendering even simple custodial care impossible, and that overcrowding remains a dangerous problem often leading to serious accidents, some of which have resulted in deaths of residents." [9]

Is the Wyatt ruling limited to state institutions like Partlow, where the conditions were shown to be shockingly bad?

No. First of all, it should be noted that although Partlow State School was a very substandard institution, experts in the *Wyatt* case testified that it was no worse than many institutions in some of our largest and richest states. But the right to habilitation applies not only to institutions where the conditions are shocking. The *Wyatt* court held that "the mentally retarded have a constitutional right to receive such individual habilitation as will give each of them a realistic opportunity to lead a more useful and meaningful life and to return to society." [10]

What are the constitutional provisions supporting the right to habilitation?

There are three basic constitutional provisions which arguably establish a right to habilitation:

Due Process: The Fourteenth Amendment states that no person shall be deprived of liberty without due process of law. This provision has been interpreted to require that governmental action affecting individual liberties be consistent with "fundamental fairness."

In many states a mentally retarded person subject to civil commitment is denied the full range of procedural safeguards made available to criminal defendants and can be confined for an indefinite term rather than for a fixed sentence. Therefore, fundamental fairness requires that something more than mere custodial confinement—i.e., habilitation—is needed to justify his loss of liberty.

Moreover, applying the due process clause to the situation of a mentally handicapped person who had been involuntarily confined, the Supreme Court has stated that the nature and duration of the commitment must bear a reasonable relationship to the purpose of that commitment.[11]

In affirming the *Wyatt* decision, the Fifth Circuit Court of Appeals accepted this substantive due process reasoning and indicated that the basic legal issue in *Wyatt* was controlled by its recent decision in *Donaldson v. O'Connor*. The Court of Appeals then briefly summarized its *Donaldson* holding as follows:

> "In *Donaldson*, we held that civilly committed mental patients have a constitutional right to such individual treatment as will help each of them to be cured or to improve his or her mental condition. We reasoned that the only permissible justifications for civil commitment, and for the massive abridgments of constitutionally protected liberties it entails, were the danger posed by the individual committed to himself or to others, or the individual's need for treatment and care. We held that where the justification for commitment was treatment, it offended the fundamentals of due process if treatment were not in fact provided; and we held that where the justification was the danger to self or to others, then treatment had to be provided as the *quid pro quo* society had to pay as the price of the extra safety it derived from the denial of individuals' liberty." [12]

Cruel and Unusual Punishment: The Eighth Amendment to the Constitution prohibits cruel and unusual punishment. The Supreme Court has held that punishing a sickness or a status, such as narcotics addiction, as if it were a criminal offense violates this prohibition.[13] Like those in the narcotics-addiction case, mentally retarded persons committed to institutions are not charged with criminal acts. Their only "offense" is a handicap which keeps them from functioning as well in some areas as the rest of us. Since civil commitment of an unwilling mentally retarded person without habilitation and training would amount to punishing him for his handicap, such commitment violates the Eighth Amendment.

Equal Protection: In many states, institutions for the mentally retarded do not come up to the standards which the state requires for other institutions in terms of fire safety, food sanitation, structural soundness and educational opportunities. By withholding from institutionalized mentally retarded persons the protections which it extends to its other citizens through the exercise of its police and *parens patriae* powers, states violate the equal protection provisions of the Fourteenth Amendment.

Does the right to habilitation apply to all residents or only to involuntary residents?

While this issue of law has not been definitively resolved, the constitutional right to habilitation would appear to apply not only to those involuntarily committed but also to at least some persons institutionalized under "voluntary" commitment. Several courts have recently questioned whether so-called "voluntary" admissions of children by their parents may not, in fact, be functionally involuntary from the children's point of view.[14]

As discussed at pp. 36-37 above, the need to provide proper training and habilitation for their mentally retarded children may put unusually heavy strains upon parents. Parents often lack the necessary skills or the money to purchase such services for their children. Unable to cope with the special demands created by the presence of a mentally retarded child, parents may be driven to a seemingly "voluntary" decision to commit the child. Commitment to an understaffed, substandard institution can be almost like locking a child in a warehouse, without any services and with virtually no stimulation. But while a parent, driven to distraction, might "voluntarily" lock a child in a warehouse, such a placement can hardly be considered voluntary on the part of the child.

A recent court decision highlights potential conflicts of interest between parents and their mentally retarded children and shows that a "voluntary" admission by a parent may in reality be an involuntary admission for the child. A three-judge Federal court in Tennessee entered an order on March 8, 1974, holding that the commitment of a person to a state mental hospital merely upon the request of a parent or guardian, with the consent of the hospital superintendent, violated the due process clause of the U.S. Constitution because of the lack of procedural safeguards to protect the interest of the child. The court ordered the state of Tennessee not to make any further commitments under the challenged statutory provisions.[15] Three-judge district courts in Pennsylvania and Georgia have recently issued similar orders.[16] Thus it may well be that persons "voluntarily" admitted to facilities for the mentally retarded, as well as those involuntarily committed, have a constitutional right to habilitation.

While limited to children, these cases raise the larger issue of whether all persons whose admissions are labeled voluntary—but who actually accept institutionalization because of coercion or lack of alternatives—might really be involuntarily committed and therefore entitled to the constitutional right to habilitation. A state statutory system giving a right to habilitation to involuntary residents but not to "voluntary" residents in the same facilities would also be highly suspect on equal protection grounds.

What if a state lacks the physical resources to implement a court order requiring minimum standards for adequate habilitation and training?

Although a lack of financial resources may be cited by administrators as a justification for failure to implement a court order requiring provision of adequate and effective habilitation, such an excuse will not be accepted where constitutional rights are involved. As the district court held in *Wyatt v. Stickney,* "failure by defendants to comply with this decree cannot be justified by a lack of operating funds. . . . [T]he unavailability of neither funds, nor staff and facilities, will justify a default by defendants in the provision of suitable treatment for the [mentally handicapped]." [17]

A distinction should be drawn between *constitutional* rights—which exist now and must be promptly vindicated—and other activities which are undertaken for the public good but which are at the discretion of the legislature and are not of constitutional dimensions. As Judge Frank Johnson explained in the *Wyatt* case:

"The responsibility for appropriate funding ultimately must fall, of course, upon the State Legislature and, to a lesser degree, upon the defendant Mental Health Board of Alabama. For the present time, the Court will defer to those bodies in hopes that they will proceed with the realization and understanding that what is involved in this case is not representative of ordinary governmental funcions such as paving roads and maintaining buildings. Rather, what is so inextricably intertwined with how the Legislature and Mental Health Board respond to the revelations of this litigation is the very preservation of human life and dignity." [18]

Of course, mental-retardation administrators and hospital superintendents often know full well that the level of habilitation and training they are providing is inadequate. Their hands are tied, however, because the legislature will not provide sufficient funding to institute needed programs. In this situation, the mental-retardation professional and administrator are caught in a frustrating dilemma. With the passage of time and the help of favorable court decisions, public opinion may persuade legislatures to increase appropriations voluntarily to provide adequate habilitation and training.

Do mentally retarded persons also have a constitutional right to protection from harm?

Yes. This was the theory under which *New York State Association for Retarded Children, Inc. v. Carey*[19]—the "Willowbrook" case—was decided.

The Willowbrook trial on the merits began October 1, 1974, and ended January 6, 1975. During that time, more than fifty witnesses appeared on the stand and nearly 3,000 pages of court testimony were recorded. Noted physicians, researchers, professors and parents appeared as witnesses and reported bruised and beaten children, maggot-infested wounds, assembly-line bathing, inadequate medical care, cruel and inappropriate use of restraints and insufficient provision of clothing at Willowbrook State School. The conclusion forced by this testimony was that the mentally retarded residents confined to Willowbrook had deteriorated physically, mentally and emotionally during their stay.

The Willowbrook lawsuit was resolved when the plaintiffs and defendants signed an extensive and detailed consent decree, which was ratified by Federal District Court Judge Orrin Judd on May 5, 1975. The decree absolutely forbids seclusion, corporal punishment, degradation, medical experimentation and the routine use of restraints. It sets as the primary goal of Willowbrook the preparation of each resident for development and life in the community at large. To this end, the decree mandates individual plans for the education, therapy, care and development of each resident.

Provisions in the decree require:

*Six scheduled hours of program activity each weekday for all residents.

*Educational programs for residents including provision for the specialized needs of the blind, deaf and multi-handicapped.

*Well-balanced nutritionally adequate diets.

*Dental services for all.

*No more than eight residents living or sleeping in a unit.

*A minimum of two hours of daily recreational activities—indoors and out—and availability of toys, books and other materials.

*Eyeglasses, hearing aids, wheelchairs and other adaptive equipment where needed.

*Adequate and appropriate clothing.

*Physicians on duty 24 hours daily for emergency cases.

*A contract with one or more accredited hospitals for acute medical care.

*A full-scale immunization program for all residents within three months.

*Compensation for voluntary labor in accordance with applicable minimum wage laws.

*Correction of health and safety hazards, including covering radiators and steam pipes to protect residents from injury, repairing broken windows and removing cockroaches and other insects and vermin.

A very important feature of the consent decree is the creation of a seven-member consumer advisory board, comprised of parents and relatives of residents, community leaders, residents and former residents, to evaluate alleged dehumanizing practices and violations of individual and legal rights.

While consent decrees ordinarily have only the status of a contractual agreement between the parties, the precedential value of Willowbrook's was substantially enhanced when the court issued a formal order ratifying the consent decree and an additional memorandum discussing the constitutional basis for the decree. In his memorandum, Judge Judd noted that:

"During the three-year course of this litigation, the fate of the mentally impaired members of our society has passed from an arcane concern to a major issue both of constitutional rights and social policy. The proposed consent judgment resolving this litigation is partly a fruit of that process.

* * *

"[The steps, standards and procedures in the consent decree] are not optimal or ideal standards, nor are they just custodial standards. They are based on the recognition that retarded persons, regardless of the degree of handicapping conditions, are capable of physical, intellectual, emotional and social growth, and . . . that a certain level of affirmative intervention and programming is necessary if that capacity for growth is to be preserved, and regression prevented.

* * *

"The consent judgment reflects the fact that protection from harm requires relief more extensive than this court originally contemplated, because harm can result not only from neglect but from conditions which cause regression or which prevent development of an individual's capabilities." [20]

In what way does the right to "protection from harm" differ from the guarantee of a "right to habilitation?"

As the Willowbrook case has shown, while these two rights are derived from separate provisions in the U.S. Constitution, the actual relief obtainable under each may be essentially the same.

Before the Willowbrook case, the "right to protection

from harm" theory, which is premised on the Eighth Amendment's prohibition against cruel and unusual punishment, had generally been regarded by advocates for the mentally retarded as less likely to provide major improvements in the conditions affecting the institutionalized retarded than their due process "right to treatment."

The reason was that historically the Eighth Amendment has been applied primarily in the prisoner-rights area. Courts measuring conditions in institutions against the prohibitions of the Eighth Amendment have traditionally acted to eliminate only conditions which are truly barbarous or inhumane or "shocking to the conscience." It was assumed, therefore, that under an Eighth Amendment standard the court might be willing to enjoin the most obviously barbarous conditions but not to order the creation of affirmative programs. After hearing extensive expert testimony, however, the Federal judge in the Willowbrook case accepted the plaintiffs' contention that in an institution for the mentally retarded it is impossible for the condition of an individual resident to remain static. Inside such institutions, without active programming the functions of the residents will inevitably deteriorate. Therefore, in order to keep residents from being harmed it is necessary to provide the full range of affirmative relief ordered under the right to habilitation in such cases as *Wyatt v. Stickney* and *Welsch v. Likins* (footnote 6 this chapter).

On the basis of this important legal precedent, advocates for the mentally retarded now have a second major constitutional theory, based upon the Eighth Amendment, which they may use as an alternative to a due process right-to-habilitation theory, based upon the Fourteenth Amendment, in seeking to improve habilitation and training services as well as safe custody for the mentally retarded.

While mentally retarded persons may be entitled to

equivalent relief under either theory, the right to protection from harm goes beyond the right to habilitation in one important respect. As discussed above, it is possible that the right to habilitation may be limited to persons who have been "involuntarily" deprived of their liberty for the purpose of habilitation. By contrast, the Willowbrook "right to protection from harm" theory would apply to any mentally retarded resident for whom the state has accepted responsibility—whether on an involuntary or a voluntary basis. Thus it is possible that the right to protection from harm, as articulated in Willowbrook, may offer relief to a larger class of the mentally retarded and may make it unnecessary to resolve the difficult legal issue as to whether "voluntary" residents have a constitutional right to habilitation.

Can legal actions really change fiscal priorities within a state services-delivery system?

Final solutions for improving the care and habilitation of the mentally retarded will not come from the courts. They must come from legislatures and from a reordering of basic fiscal priorities. The evidence suggests that lawsuits such as *Wyatt* and the Willowbrook case can be valuable catalysts, serving to hold administrators accountable and generally to focus public attention on the denial of the constitutional rights of this underrepresented and oft-forgotten group. For example, largely as the result of the litigation in Alabama, the budget of that state's Department of Mental Health has gone from the $28 million given it by the state legislature in 1970 to an estimated $83 million in 1975. And as a result of initial testimony about Partlow State School, the *Wyatt* court issued an emergency order to protect the lives of Partlow inmates during the course of the case. The court ordered the state to hire 300 new aide-level employees within 30 days and gave the state permission to bypass civil service procedures which might delay hiring. Within 10 days after this order was made public, more than 1000 persons had applied for jobs and the quota was met.

To give another example, according to Bruce Ennis, one of the attorneys for plaintiffs in the Willowbrook case, as a result of the 1975 consent decree, the state of New York will be spending approximately $40 million more for Willowbrook this year than it was spending in 1972 when the lawsuit was filed.

What Federal statute provides a right to habilitation and a right to protection from harm for mentally retarded persons?

Section 201 of the Developmentally Disabled Assistance and Bill of Rights Act,[21] which was signed by President Ford on October 4, 1975, provides:

"Sec. III. Congress makes the following findings respecting the rights of persons with developmental disabilities:

"(1) Persons with developmental disabilities have a right to appropriate treatment, services, and habilitation for such disabilities.

* * *

"(3) The Federal Government and the States both have an obligation to assure that public funds are not provided to any institutional or other residential programs for persons with developmental disabilities that—

"(A) does not provide treatment, services, and habilitation which is appropriate to the needs of such persons; or

"(B) does not meet the following minimum standards:

"(i) Provision of a nourishing, well-balanced daily diet to the persons with developmental disabilities being served by the program.

"(ii) Provision to such persons of appropriate and sufficient medical and dental services.

"(iii) Prohibition of the use of physical restraint on such persons unless absolutely necessary and prohibition of the use of such restraint as a punishment or as a substitute for a habilitation program.

"(iv) Prohibition on the excessive use of chemical restraints on such persons and the use of such restraints as punishment or as a substitute for a habilitation program or in quantities that interfere with services, treatment, or habilitation for such persons.

"(v) Permission for close relatives of such persons to visit them at reasonable hours without prior notice.

"(vi) Compliance with adequate fire and safety standards as may be promulgated by the Secretary [of Health, Education and Welfare]."

The act also places increased emphasis on deinstitutionalization, primarily by requiring states to use at least 10 percent of their formula-grant allotment in fiscal 1976 and at least 30 percent in each succeeding fiscal year for development and implementation of plans designed to eliminate inappropriate institutional placements.[22]

NOTES

1. Although they are sometimes used interchangeably, the terms "right to habilitation," "right to treatment" and "right to education" actually denote separate, though

related legal concepts. *Habilitation* is the process of achieving the highest possible level of personal functioning. As used by the court in *Wyatt v. Stickney,* habilitation is:

> "the process by which the staff of the institution assists the resident to acquire and maintain those life skills which enable him to cope more effectively with the demands of his own person and of his environment and to raise the level of his physical, mental, and social efficiency. Habilitation includes but is not limited to programs of formal, structured education and treatment." 344 F. Supp. 387, 395 (M.D. Ala. 1972), *aff'd in part, remanded in part sub nom. Wyatt v. Aderholt,* 503 F.2d 1305 (5th Cir. 1974).

Treatment refers to therapeutic or curative procedures administered to persons under a medical model. When used in connection with mentally retarded persons, it refers primarily to physiological (as opposed to psychological) procedures. For example, the *Wyatt* court used "treatment" to denote "the prevention, amelioration and/or cure of a resident's physical disabilities or illnesses." *Id. Education* is a specific method of habilitation through formal training and instruction.

2. *See, e.g.,* Ohio Rev. Code Ann. §5123.85 (Page Supp. 1974).

3. *Wyatt v. Stickney,* 344 F. Supp. 387, 395 (M.D.Ala. 1972), *aff'd in part, remanded in part sub nom. Wyatt v. Aderholt,* 503 F.2d 1305 (5th Cir. 1974).

4. *Donaldson v. O'Connor,* 493 F.2d 507 (5th Cir. 1974), *aff'd in part, remanded in part,* 422 U.S. 563 (1975).

5. *Horacek v. Exon,* 357 F. Supp. 71 (D. Neb. 1973) (preliminary order), consent decree entered August 1975.

6. *Welsch v. Likins,* 373 F. Supp. 487 (D. Minn. 1974).

7. *Ricci v. Greenblatt,* Civil Action No. 72-469-T (D. Mass., Nov. 12, 1973) (consent decree).

8. *Saville v. Treadway,* Civil Action No. Nashville 6969

(M.D. Tenn., Mar. 8, 1974), consent decree entered Sept. 18, 1974.

9. *Wyatt v. Stickney, supra,* Unpublished Interim Emergency Order, March 2, 1972.

10. 344 F. Supp. at 390.

11. *Jackson v. Indiana,* 406 U.S. 715, 738 (1972).

12. 503 F.2d at 1312. On appeal to the U.S. Supreme Court the Fifth Circuit *Donaldson* decision was vacated (see pp. 91-92), but *Wyatt* remains the law of the Fifth Circuit.

13. *Robinson v. California,* 370 U.S. 660 (1962).

14. *See Horacek v. Exon, supra* note 5, 357 F. Supp. at 74; *Saville v. Treadway, supra* note 8; *Bartley v. Kremens,* 402 F. Supp. 1039 (E.D. Pa. 1975), *stay granted,* 96 S.Ct. 558, *probable jurisdiction noted,* 96 S.Ct. 1457 (March 22, 1976); *New York State Ass'n for Retarded Children, Inc. v. Rockefeller,* 357 F. Supp. 752, 762 (E.D. N.Y.1973) (preliminary injunction); *J. L. v. Parham,* —F.Supp.—, No. 75-163 M.A.C. (M.D. Ga. 1976), *stay granted,* 96 S. Ct. 1503 (1976).

15. *Saville v. Treadway, supra* note 8.

16. *Bartley v. Kremens* and *J. L. v. Parham, supra* note 14.

17. *Wyatt v. Stickney,* 344 F. Supp. 373, 377 (M.D. Ala. 1972), *aff'd in part, remanded in part sub nom. Wyatt v. Aderholt,* 503 F.2d 1305 (5th Cir. 1974) (companion case on the mentally ill).

18. *Id.*

19. 393 F. Supp. 715 (E.D.N.Y.1975) (consent decree approved).

20. 393 F. Supp. at 717-18.

21. Pub. L. No. 94-103, 89 Stat. 486, §201 (Oct. 4, 1975), *to be codified at* 42 U.S.C. §6010. Sections 202 and 203 of the Act require the states to put into effect habilitation plans and to protect and advocate the rights of persons with developmental disabilities in order to receive Federal funds. These sections will be codified at 42 U.S.C. §§6011-12.

22. Pub. L. No. 94-103, 89 Stat. 486, §§110(b), 111(a) (Oct. 4, 1975), *to be codified* at 42 U.S.C. §6062-63.

LIMITATIONS ON HAZARDOUS, INTRUSIVE AND EXPERIMENTAL PROCEDURES

Do competent mentally retarded persons in institutions have a right to refuse potentially hazardous or intrusive procedures such as sterilization?

Traditionally, decisions about therapies or medical procedures have been within the unfettered discretion of the habilitation professional responsible for a mentally retarded resident's program. Recently, however, concern has arisen about imposition of potentially hazardous or intrusive procedures upon objecting recipients. There are attempts being made to sketch out the conditions under which even involuntarily committed mentally retarded persons might refuse particular treatments. Recent legal developments suggest that competent mentally retarded persons may have a right to refuse such treatments.

What are the legal bases for the right of competent residents to refuse hazardous or intrusive procedures?

The legal bases for the right to refuse may be derived in whole or in part from the statutory law, the common law and the Federal and state constitutions.

Although most procedures remain unregulated by statute, a number of states have recently passed laws which limit the imposition of certain treatment procedures by requiring the informed consent of persons in institutions. The most frequently regulated procedures are psychosurgery, surgery and electroconvulsive therapy.[1] Administrative rules and regulations may also provide a basis for a right to refuse. Since states have differing statutes, rules and regulations, it is impossible to generalize as to the limitations which exist now or may be imposed in the future. But there is a trend toward increased regulation.

The common law protects the inviolability of individuals. As Justice Cardoza once wrote, "Every human being of adult years and sound mind has a right to determine what shall be done with his own body. . . ."[2] Under existing tort law, consent is the mechanism by which a mentally retarded resident would grant a professional permission to invade his person for the purposes of treatment. Informed consent is necessary to distinguish legally permissible intrusions from those which would subject the therapist to liability for an unauthorized "offensive touching" or assault and battery on his patient. These common-law protections apply both in and out of institutions. Traditionally, however, various privileges and immunities have made it legally permissible for mental-health professionals to use treatment procedures on mentally retarded persons in institutions even without informed consent.

Constitutional guarantees which may impose limitations upon enforced therapy are: the right to physical and mental privacy and autonomy, the prohibition against cruel and unusual punishment and the right to due process.

Where exactly does the United States Constitution provide a right of competent residents to refuse hazardous or intrusive procedures?

While the Constitution nowhere explicitly provides limits upon enforced therapy, such limits may be extrapolated from other recognized constitutional protections.

The Right to Physical and Mental Privacy and Autonomy: An early assertion of the right to privacy was in Justice Brandeis' now-famous dissent in *Olmstead v. United States.*[3] Noting in 1928 that "[a]dvances in the psychic and related sciences may bring means of exploring unexpressed beliefs, thoughts, and emotions," he maintained that, "[the makers of our Constitution] sought to protect Americans in their beliefs, their thoughts, their emotions and their sensations. They conferred, as against the Government, the right to be let alone—the most comprehensive of rights and the right most valued by civilized men." [4] The concept of a right to privacy has recently been greatly advanced by the Supreme Court in such decisions as *Griswold v. Connecticut*,[5] and *Roe v. Wade*,[6] protecting an individual's rights to privacy in the use of contraceptives and in obtaining abortions, respectively.

Closely related to the right to mental privacy is the right to mental autonomy. This is an aspect of the First Amendment's protection of free speech. If the First Amendment protects the communication of ideas, the theory goes, it must necessarily protect a person's autonomy to generate thoughts which are the predicate to speech.[7] In at least two recent cases, lower courts have recognized a right to mental privacy and autonomy which would protect mentally retarded persons and others, both in and out of institutions, from certain state intrusions.[8] According to a three-judge state court in *Kaimowitz v. Michigan Department of Mental Health*:

> "A person's mental processes, the communication of ideas, and the generation of ideas come within the ambit of the First Amendment. To the extent the First Amendment protects the dissemination of ideas and the expression of thoughts, it equally must protect the individual's right to generate ideas. . . .
>
> * * *
>
> "There is no privacy more deserving of constitutional protection than that of one's mind. . . . Intrusion into one's intellect, when one is

involuntarily detained and subject to the control of institutional authorities, is an intrusion into one's constitutionally protected right of privacy. If one is not protected in his thoughts, behavior, personality and identity, then the right of privacy becomes meaningless." [9]

In *Mackey v. Procunier*,[10] the Ninth Circuit Court of Appeals expressed a similar view. Mackey alleged that while in prison, without his consent, he was administered succinycholine, a breath-stopping and paralyzing "fright drug," as part of an experiment to ascertain whether by evoking fright and inflicting pain, accompanied by psychological suggestion, "bad" behavior patterns could be affected.[11] Reversing a lower court's dismissal of Mackey's complaint, the Court of Appeals asserted that

"Proof of [his allegations] could . . . raise serious constitutional questions respecting . . . impermissible tinkering with the mental processes." [12]

The Right to Be Free from Cruel and Unusual Punishment: Another limitation upon the power of the state to impose procedures upon unwilling persons is the Eighth Amendment's proscription of cruel and unusual punishment. In *Wheeler v. Glass*, for example, the Seventh Circuit held that the binding of two institutionalized mentally retarded children in spread-eagle position for 77½ hours as punishment for breaking the institution's rules constituted a violation of the Eighth Amendment.[13]

A recent Eighth Circuit Court of Appeals decision suggests that the Eighth Amendment may also protect mentally retarded persons from certain forms of enforced "treatments" which have been imposed over their objection and which are really punishments in disguise. In *Knecht v. Gillman*,[14] two residents of the

Iowa Security Medical Facility sought to enjoin the use of apomorphine, a vomiting-inducing drug, which they said was used as part of an aversive-conditioning program for residents with behavioral problems. The court ruled that imposition of this procedure without informed consent would be cruel and unusual punishment, and noted that "the mere characterization of an act as 'treatment' does not insulate it from eighth amendment scrutiny." [15]

The Right Not to Be Deprived of Life, Liberty or Property Without Due Process of Law: The Fourteenth Amendment provides that no state shall "deprive any person of life, liberty or property, without due process of law." Denying mentally retarded residents such basics as food, beds, use of personal property, recreation and personal clothing, even as part of a "therapeutic" token-economy program, might well constitute deprivation of liberty and property and require due process.[16] Where the liberty or property interests involved are important ones, due process will be violated unless the resident has either given informed consent to the intrusive procedure or unless the government can justify the intrusion both as necessary to promote a compelling government purpose[17] and as no more intrusive than necessary to promote that purpose.[18]

What are the necessary components of informed consent to a hazardous or intrusive procedure?

For consent to a therapy or medical procedure to be valid, it must be competent, knowledgeable and voluntary. A mentally retarded person lacks the competency or capacity to consent if he cannot understand and knowingly make a decision based upon relevant information or if for any other reason he cannot manifest his consent. For consent to be "knowledgeable," a person should have all the information concerning the proposed procedure which he reasonably needs to know in order to make an intelligent decision. Such information would certainly include the nature of the proposed procedure; its likelihood of success; the likelihood, nature, extent and duration of any positive impacts, harms or side effects; the reasonable alternative procedures available; and an explanation as to why the specific procedure recommended is the procedure of choice. In order to assure that the decision is truly voluntary, the person should be informed orally and in writing that no benefits or penalties will be contingent upon his agreement or refusal to undergo the proposed procedure. More specifically, there must be an explicit oral and written understanding by an institutional resident that his consent is not a precondition for release from the institution, that his decision should not be made to obtain approval from or to avoid reprisals from the staff, and that he is free to withdraw consent at any point, without penalty.

What protections against hazardous or intrusive treatments or medical procedures does an incompetent institutionalized resident have?

Where a mentally retarded resident is incompetent to make a decision about whether to undergo a particular procedure, some form of substitute decision-making must take place. Ordinarily, the vicarious decision-maker would be a relative or guardian. But because hazardous or intrusive procedures may infringe fundamental First, Eighth or Fourteenth Amendment rights, additional protections—such as review by an independent "human rights committee"—would seem to be required to insure that the procedures imposed are in the "best interest" of the retarded person and are no more intrusive than necessary to accomplish the legitimate therapeutic or behavioral goal.

For example, as the *Wyatt* court stated in a recent order regulating hazardous and intrusive procedures,

"It must be emphasized at the outset of this order that, in setting forth the minimum constitutional requiremens for the employment of certain extraordinary or potentially hazardous modes of treatment, the Court is not undertaking to determine which forms of treatment are appropriate in particular situations. Such a diagnostic decision is a medical judgment and is not within the province, jurisdiction or expertise of this Court. But the determination of what procedural safeguards must accompany the use of extraordinary or potentially hazardous modes of treatment on patients in the state's mental institutions is a fundamentally legal question." [19]

What rights do institutionalized mentally retarded persons have to protection in human experimentation?

Competent mentally retarded persons have the same constitutional right to refuse risky experimental procedures as they do to refuse hazardous and intrusive procedures in general. The Constitution also protects an incompetent mentally retarded person from risky human experimentation unless such experimentation is demonstrably in his best interest.

In addition, the Department of Health, Education and Welfare has promulgated final department-wide regulations for the general protection of human research subjects,[20] and has issued a proposed policy requiring additional protections pertaining to activities involving the institutionalized mentally disabled as subjects.[21]

Under the general HEW regulations in effect, no activity involving human subjects to be supported by the Department of HEW shall be undertaken unless an institutional review board of the organization has reviewed and approved such activity and the institution has submitted to HEW a certification of such review and approval. This review shall determine whether the subjects will be placed at risk and, if risk is involved, whether:

"(1) The risks to the subject are so outweighed by the sum of the benefit to the subject and the importance of the knowledge to be gained as to warrant a decision to allow the subject to accept these risks;

"(2) The rights and welfare of any such subjects will be adequately protected; and

"(3) Legally effective informed consent will be obtained by adequate and appropriate methods in accordance with the provisions of this part . . ."

Where the board finds risk involved, it must review the conduct of the activity at timely intervals.

Under HEW general policy, "[n]o grant or contract involving human subjects at risk shall be made to an individual unless he is affiliated with or sponsored by an institution which can and does assume responsibility for the subjects involved."

Additional safeguards for the protection of the institutionalized mentally disabled would be provided under proposed HEW policy. As used in this proposed policy, the term "institutionalized mentally disabled individuals" includes but is not limited to residents in public or private mental hospitals, community mental health centers and general hospitals and mentally disabled individuals who reside in halfway houses or in nursing homes. Institutionalized mentally disabled individuals may not be included in human experimentation unless

"(a) The proposed activity is related to the etiology, pathogenesis, prevention, diagnosis, or treatment of mental disability or the management, training, or rehabilitation of the mentally disabled and seeks information which cannot be obtained from subjects who are not institutionalized mentally disabled;

"(b) The individual's legally effective informed consent to participation in the activity or, where the individual is legally incompetent, the informed consent of a representative with legal authority so to consent on behalf of the individual has been obtained; and

"(c) The individual's assent to such participation has also been secured, when in the judgment of the consent committee he or she has sufficient mental capacity to understand what is proposed and to express an opinion as to his or her participation."

The effective and proposed HEW regulations governing human experimentation upon institutionalized mentally disabled persons would further require establishment of an organizational review committee, a consent committee, confidentiality in record-keeping and regular reporting concerning human experimentation.

While HEW was promulgating the regulations described above, Congress took independent action to protect subjects of human experimentation by amending the Public Health Service Act to establish a "National Commission for the Protection of Human Subjects of Biomedical and Behavioral Research." [22] This commission, which has a two-year life, is charged with conducting a comprehensive investigation and study to identify the basic ethical principles which should govern the conduct of biomedical reserch involving human subjects; developing appropriate guidelines; and, more specifically, with identifying the requirements for informed consent to participation in biomedical and behavioral research by the "institutionalized mentally inferior."

NOTES

1. *See, e.g.,* Alaska Stat. §47.30.130 (1975) (consent required for surgery and psychiatric therapies); Cal. Welf. & Inst'ns Code §§5325(f)-(g) (West Supp. 1975) (right to refuse shock treatment and psychosurgery, including lobotomy); Conn. Stat. Ann. §17-206d(1975) (no medical or surgical procedures, including electroshock therapy, may be performed without consent).

2. *Schloendorff v. Society of The New York Hosp.,* 211 N.Y. 125, 129, 105 N.E. 92, 93 (1914).

3. 277 U.S. 438, 471 (1928). The majority opinion was later overruled by *Katz v. United States,* 389 U.S. 347 (1967).

4. *Id.* at 474, 478.

5. 381 U.S. 479 (1965).

6. 410 U.S. 113 (1973).

7. *See, e.g., Whitney v. California,* 274 U.S. 357, 375 (1927) (Brandeis, J., concurring); *Stanley v. Georgia,* 394 U.S. 557, 565 (1969). *Whitney,* like *Olmstead, supra,* note 3, was subsequently overruled. *Brandenburg v. Ohio,* 395 U.S. 444 (1969).

8. While the first of these cases concerned a committed sex-psychopath who was to have been the subject of experimental psychosurgery, and the second a prisoner, the precedential effect of both is relevant for other institutionalized persons, including the mentally retarded.

9. *Kaimowitz v. Michigan Dept. of Mental Health,* Civil Action No. 73-19434-AW (Wayne County, Mich. Cir. Ct., July 10, 1973), sl. op. at 32 and 38; *reported in part at* 42 U.S.L.W. 2063, 2064.

10. 477 F.2d 877 (9th Cir. 1973).

11. *Id.* at 878 n. 1.

12. *Id.* at 878 (footnotes omitted).

13. 473 F.2d 983, 987 (7th Cir. 1973).

14. 488 F.2d 1136 (8th Cir. 1973).

15. *Id.* at 1139.

16. *See Meyer v. Nebraska,* 262 U.S. 390, 399 (1923); *Wyatt v. Stickney,* 344 F. Supp. 373 and 344 F. Supp. 387 (M.D. Ala. 1972), *aff'd in part, remanded in part sub nom. Wyatt v. Aderholt,* 503 F.2d 1035 (5th Cir. 1974).

17. *See, e.g., Wisconsin v. Yoder,* 406 U.S. 205, 214-15, 221-29 (1972).

18. *See Griswold v. Connecticut,* 381 U.S. 479, 485 (1965); *Shelton v. Tucker,* 364 U.S. 479, 488 (1960). While the constitutional guarantees of autonomy and privacy, protection from cruel and unusual punishment and due process serve as the primary bases for a right to refuse certain procedures, other constitutional bases are worthy of mention. In certain instances, imposition of procedures will violate the First Amendment's guarantee of freedom of religion. *Winters v. Miller,* 446 F.2d 65 (2d Cir.), *cert. denied,* 404 U.S. 985 (1971). Moreover, the nature and degree of deprivations in certain token-economy programs may be limited by several different constitutional provisions. Among the constitutionally guaranteed rights which such programs may violate are the right of worship, the right to send and receive correspondence and printed materials and the right of access to the courts. Still other possible theoretical bases for a right to refuse treatment are the equal protection clause and the Fourth Amendment. However, neither of these latter two approaches has yet been raised effectively in litigation.

19. Unpublished Order, Civil Action No. 3195-N (M.D. Ala., Feb. 28, 1975).

20. 45 C.F.R. §§46.101-.122(1975).

21. 39 Fed. Reg. 30648, 30652, 30655-56 (1974).

22. Pub. L. No. 93-348, §§201-05 (July 12, 1974), *codified in Short Title Note to* 42 U.S.C. §289.1 (Supp. IV, 1974).

THE RIGHT TO SEXUAL EXPRESSION

Do mentally retarded persons in institutions have a right to sexual expression?

Mentally retarded persons—whether institutionalized or not—have a right to sexual expression. In spite of this, many institutions attempt to restrain sexual expression by retarded residents.

Many retardation facilities have sexually segregated day and/or dormitory areas. Free time does not often, at least explicitly, include permission to engage in sexual activity. However, unsanctioned sexual activity among mentally retarded residents does in fact occur and many institutional staff members admit its existence. Administrative efforts to dampen sexual activity are frequently couched in terms of administrative convenience or protection of residents. The former justification is simply insufficient as grounds for interfering with a basic human right. And the rationale that sexual relations among mentally retarded residents may not be truly voluntary and may involve coercion or abuse is like burning down the house to roast the pig: It leads to overly restrictive measures for an entire insitutional population when the actual problem may involve only a few identifiable persons.

Not surprisingly, the courts are reluctant to become involved with such a delicate issue. But at least one court has recognized that the right to sexual expression belongs to the mentally retarded, as to all other citizens. In its decision on adequate institutional care for the mentally retarded, a Federal court in Alabama has ordered that "the institution shall provide, with adequate supervision suitable opportunities for the patient's interaction with members of the opposite sex." [1]

Are mentally retarded persons in institutions entitled to receive sex education and birth control substances?

Yes. The rights to education and habilitation (see pages 104 and 57-73) include the right to receive information about sex and contraception. Because these topics are sometimes considered "inflammatory" or "improper," however, they are frequently avoided. Generally, the availability of sex education and birth control counseling to retarded residents is determined by the administrative policies of the particular institution, not by law.

Do institutionalized mentally retarded persons have rights to marry, procreate and have children?

Yes. For a discussion of the legal issues involved, see pages 113-124.

NOTE

1. *Wyatt v. Stickney,* 344 F. Supp. 387, 399 (M.D. Ala. 1972), *aff'd in part, remanded in part sub nom. Wyatt v. Aderholt,* 503 F.2d 1305 (5th Cir. 1974). The court does, however, provide an exception "where a Qualified Mental Retardation Professional responsible for the formulation of a particular resident's habilitation plan writes an order to the contrary and explains the reasons therefor." *Id.*

THE RIGHT TO FAIR COMPENSATION FOR INSTITUTIONAL LABOR

What is "institutional peonage"?

"Institutional peonage" describes the formerly widespread practice of employing residents in institutions for the mentally retarded to perform productive labor associated with the maintenance of the institution, without adequate compensation.[1] A 1972 study of 154 institutions in 47 states, which represented 76 percent of existing facilities for the mentally retarded, found that 32,180 of 150,000 residents were participating in work programs. Thirty percent were receiving no payment at all and an additional 50 percent were receiving less than $10 per week.[2]

In many state institutions, cleaning, laundering, kitchen work, waiting tables and preparing food, maintenance housekeeping and care of other residents have traditionally been performed in large measure by working residents. In exchange for this labor, working residents might be given open-ward privileges or some other "symbolic" reward; they are virtually never paid the prevailing wage. Institutional peonage exists in part because, given their understaffing and underfinancing, our institutions can't afford to pay regular employees for the work which is necessary to run them.

Aside from exploitative motives, such nonremunerated work has traditionally been allowed because of difficulties in distinguishing between work which is primarily for the benefit of the institution and work which is chiefly for the benefit of the resident. Uncompensated labor injures resident-workers in a number of ways beyond the obvious loss of income. They are denied work-related benefits such as workman's compensation and state retirement plans. They are denied the therapeutic benefits of appropriate monetary rewards. Perhaps most significantly, working residents who are not paid for their labor often perceive themselves to be exploited or enslaved and thereby lose a basic sense of self-respect and dignity which is both their right as human beings and a vital element of any meaningful habilitation program.

How are residents forced to work?

Most institutions for the retarded would maintain

that they do not force their residents to work. But, as is widely recognized, there are many pressures in institutions which coerce residents to perform institution-maintaining work and to conform to other institutional norms. A resident's refusal to work often results in staff antagonism, restriction of ground privileges or increased medication. It is common for the resident to be labelled uncooperative—with bad effects on his efforts to be released—when he fails to participate in a "voluntary" work program.

What recent court decision has prohibited institutional peonage?

A major step in the abolition of institutional peonage was the decision of the United States District Court for the District of Columbia in *Souder v. Brennan*.[3] This ruling stated that the 1966 Amendments to the Fair Labor Standards Act extending the minimum-wage and overtime provisions to all employees of "hospitals, institutions and schools for the mentally handicapped," applied to resident workers. The *Souder* court also held that the United States Department of Labor must undertake reasonable enforcement activity on behalf of resident-workers. Addressing the Department of Labor's defense that it is very difficult to distinguish between work and vocational training, the court in *Souder v. Brennan* noted,

"Economic reality is the test of employment and the reality is that many of the patient-workers perform work for which they are in no way handicapped and from which the institution derives full economic benefit. So long as the institution derives any consequential economic benefit the economic reality test would indicate an employment relationship rather than mere therapeutic exercise." [4]

Final regulations concerning "employment of patient-workers in hospitals and institutions at sub-minimum wages" were published on February 7, 1975.[5] These regulations, covering employment of patients whose earning or productive capacity is impaired, allow employers to pay such workers a pro rata share of the full minimum wage adjusted to the actual productivity of the handicapped worker relative to that of a "regular" employee.

As this book goes to press, the United States Supreme Court's decision in *National League of Cities v. Usery* [6] appears to limit significantly the reach of the *Souder* decision. In *National League of Cities,* a consortium of states successfully argued that the Federal government's attempt to regulate the minimum wage in state-operated facilities was an unconstitutional intrusion upon state sovereignty. Therefore mentally retarded workers in state-run facilities, just like their nonretarded co-workers, are no longer guaranteed a Federal minimum wage, although they are still entitled to the state minimum wage. However, because *National League of Cities* pertains only to state employees, the Fair Labor Standards Act and the *Souder* decision still apply to mentally retarded residents working in private facilities.

Are institutions entitled to recover back wages paid to working residents as payment for room, board and treatment?

The law is at present unclear as to whether institutions may assess residents for the cost of their room, board and treatment.[7] But even if so, residents should be entitled to keep at least a significant part of their earnings. While many states provide in their civil-commitment statutes that the resident or his relatives must contribute to the cost of institutionalization according to ability to pay, there is often an income-cutoff point below which no assessments are levied.

Thus, if an institutional resident earns less than $4,000 or $5,000 a year, there is often no obligation to pay any part of the costs of institutionalization. Many residents, even if paid the minimum wage for work performed, would never reach the minimum-income level at which these state statutes would require them to pay for their institutionalization: other residents even after statutorily mandated assessments for room, board and treatment based upon income would have a residuum of their earnings from work to be spent as they wished. Under yet another set of possible circumstances, residents who have savings or other sources of income may already be meeting their statutory obligations as to the cost of their institutionalization and would therefore be entitled to receive their earnings from work free and clear.

Moreover, even where institutions are entitled to recover wages for room, board and treatment, such charges should be carefully scrutinized. The actual cost of the room and board in many of our large state warehousing institutions is very small and charges for "habilitation" will often be especially vulnerable to challenge. Many institutions figure the cost of providing care and habilitation by dividing the number of residents into the total costs of the institution—which include overhead and all administrative staff. Where institutions seek to recover back charges for habilitation, they should be made to prove that they are actually providing such habilitation services. To charge residents for habilitation when no habilitation is actually provided—and when the habilitation figure is derived from overhead and administrative costs—is fraudulent.

Finally, under present Department of Labor regulations,[8] the resident-worker must receive his wages free and clear. Only afterwards may the facility attempt to recover any monies for services to which it is legally entitled.

NOTES

1. *See generally* Friedman, "The Mentally Handicapped Citizen and Institutional Labor," 87 *Harv. L. Rev.* 567 (1974). "Institutional peonage" is to be distinguished from vocational-training tasks not involving the operation or maintenance of the institution and from personal-housekeeping tasks, such as the making of one's own bed.
2. J. Richardson, *A Survey of the Present Status of Vocational Training in State-Supported Institutions for the Mentally Retarded* 4, 11-12, July 18, 1974 (written for Dr. I. Ignacy Goldberg, Columbia University Teachers College).
3. 367 F. Supp. 808 (D.D.C. 1973).
4. *Id.* at 813 (footnotes omitted).
5. 29 C.F.R. §§ 529.1-.17 (1975).
6. — U.S. —, 44 U.S.L.W. 4974 (June 24, 1976).
7. While it seems possible that to confine residents and then require them to pay for their room, board and treatment might be a violation of due process or equal protection, the courts that have ruled on this question to date have generally held that it is constitutionally permissible for the state to make such charges.
8. 29 C.F.R. §529.4 (i) (1975).

THE RIGHT TO LIBERTY

Do mentally retarded persons have a constitutional right to liberty?

Yes, at least under some circumstances. The leading case on this issue is the U.S. Supreme Court's historic decision in *O'Connor v. Donaldson.*[1] Although this case involved an allegedly mentally ill plaintiff, it is discussed here because it strongly suggests that the mentally retarded also have a constitutional right to liberty.

Kenneth Donaldson had been civilly committed to the Florida State Hospital at Chattahoochee in January 1955, diagnosed as "paranoid schizophrenic." He remained in that hospital for the next 14½ years, during which he received little or no psychiatric treatment. Donaldson contended that he had a constitutional right either to be treated or to be released from the state hospital.

Although the *Donaldson* case was upheld in the lower court on the theory that involuntarily confined mental patients have a right to treatment or release the Supreme Court found that it was not necessary to decide this claim to affirm the decision. Instead the Supreme Court focused on the constitutional right to liberty.

The narrow legal holding of *Donaldson* is that "a state cannot constitutionally confine without more a non-dangerous individual who is capable of surviving safely in freedom by himself or with the help of willing and responsible family members and friends."

Writing for the unanimous court, Justice Stewart rejected the notion that mental patients might be exiled by a community which finds their presence upsetting:

"May the State fence in the harmless mentally ill solely to save its citizens from exposure to those whose ways are different? One might as well ask if the State, to avoid public unease, could incarcerate all who are physically unattractive or socially eccentric. Mere public intolerance or animosity cannot constitutionally justify the deprivation of . . . physical liberty. . . . That the State has a proper interest in providing care and assistance to the unfortunate goes without saying. But the mere presence of mental illness does not disqualify a person from preferring his home to the comforts of an institution."

While the *Donaldson* case was decided narrowly, the opinion is rich in ancillary holdings. For example, the court noted that states are under a continuing obligation to review periodically the justifications for individual commitments, and that mental-health personnel *can* be held personally liable for bad-faith violations of a patient's constitutional right to liberty.

As for its implications for the mentally retarded, *Donaldson* is noteworthy as the first Supreme Court opinion in recent times to discuss the rights of a *civilly committed* person who has not been accused or convicted of a crime. A unanimous court has now expressed concern for the plight of the mentally handicapped in our country and has recognized them as citizens with the same full constitutional rights as the rest of us.

The *Donaldson* decision does not, however, directly address issues of primary concern to mentally retarded persons and their advocates. Language in the *Donaldson* decision could certainly be relied upon by mentally retarded persons who are not dangerous and are able to function in society but whom the state wished to commit. But whereas Kenneth Donaldson was confined over his objections, many mentally retarded persons enter institutions in the hope of receiving meaningful habilitation and training. The main focus of concern for mentally retarded persons is not with liberty *per se*, but (1) with whether the Constitution provides some basic right to habilitation and training (an issue expressly left undecided in the *Donaldson* opinion) and (2) if so, whether the mentally retarded have a right to receive such habilitation and training in more normal, community-based facilities rather than in remote institutions. These issues have been and continue to be before the lower courts in the landmark right-to-habilitation and right-to-education cases discussed elsewhere in this book.

NOTE

1. 422 U.S. 563 (1975).

OTHER BASIC RIGHTS IN INSTITUTIONS

What other basic rights do mentally retarded persons have in institutions?

As an aspect of their constitutional right to habilitation, the *Wyatt* court found that mentally retarded residents in institutions had a constitutional right to a humane physical and psychological environment. The court found that residents had a right to dignity, privacy and humane care and held that residents shall lose none of the rights enjoyed by citizens of Alabama and of the United States solely by reason of their admission or commitment to institutions. The court then went on to enumerate a whole series of other rights. These other rights are fully set forth in the *Wyatt* and Willowbrook cases. As noted at pp. 70-71, the Developmentally Disabled Assistance and Bill of Rights Act contains similar provisions.

Other such bills of rights are now being provided under progressive state statutes. For example, Florida has recently enacted a "Bill of Rights of Retarded Persons"[1] which spells out and guarantees thirteen basic rights for clients of the state mental-retardation system. The clients' rights enumerated in the new law (effective July 1, 1975) include dignity, privacy and humane care; religious freedom; an "unrestricted" right to communication and visitation; possession and use of personal clothes and belongings; education and training services (though not at any particular level), including sex education; behavioral and leisure-time activities; physical exercise; humane discipline; and compensation for labor in accordance with applicable Federal regulations.

Additionally, clients are guaranteed the right to "prompt and appropriate medical treatment . . . consistent with the accepted standards of medical practice in the community." This section also includes some limitations on administration of medication; for example, it requires all prescriptions to have a termination date, although it does not set a maximum duration for such prescriptions. Further, medication is not to be used as punishment or as a substitute for programming, and drug regimens are to be reviewed at least semiannually. The new law also requires express and informed consent from the client, if competent, or else the parent or legal guardian for both necessary surgical procedures and "experimental medical treatment." Under the new Florida statute, treatment programs involving use of "noxious or painful stimuli" are absolutely prohibited, while programs to eliminate "bizarre or unusual" behaviors must be preceded by a physical examination to rule out organic causes. Physical restraints are to be used only in emergencies to protect the client from imminent injury to himself or others; totally enclosed cribs and barred enclosures are considered to be restraints subject to this limitation.

NOTE

1. The Bill of Rights of Retarded Persons, Fla. Stat. Ann. §393.13 (Supp. 1975).

IV

Rights of Mentally Retarded Persons in the Community

THE RIGHT TO EDUCATION

Why have advocates for the mentally retarded placed special emphasis on the right to education?

For the same reasons that education [1] is regarded as so important by our society. Educational opportunity has long been recognized as the primary vehicle for social and economic advancement. Without access to education, other rights—such as the freedoms of speech, religion and association and the right peaceably to assemble and to petition the government—are diminished, perhaps entirely nullified. As the Supreme Court held in its historic decision in *Brown v. Board of Education:*

> "Today, education is perhaps the most important function of state and local governments. Compulsory school attendance laws and the great expenditures for education both demonstrate our recognition of the importance of education to our democratic society. It is required in the performance of our most basic public responsibilities, even service in the armed forces. It is the very foundation of good citizenship. Today, it is a

principal instrument in awakening the child to cultural values, in preparing him for later professional training, and in helping him to adjust normally to his environment. In these days, it is doubtful that any child may reasonably be expected to succeed in life if he is denied the opportunity of an education." [2]

The court was not considering the problems of handicapped children in the *Brown* case. Yet its rationale as applied to such children becomes even more compelling, since the handicapped child may be completely dependent on skills which only an education can provide.

Can mentally retarded persons benefit from public education?

Yes. This issue was the subject of extensive expert testimony in the right-to-education test case that was the first important breakthrough for legal activists seeking to articulate the rights of the mentally retarded. As the parties' consent agreement in the case stated:

"Expert testimony in this action indicates that all mentally retarded persons are capable of benefiting from a program of education and training; that the greatest number of retarded persons, given such education and training, are capable of achieving self-sufficiency, and the remaining few, with such education and training, are capable of achieving some degree of self-care; that the earlier such education and training begins, the more thoroughly and the more efficiently a mentally retarded person will benefit from it; and, whether begun early or not, that a mentally retarded person can benefit at any point in his life and development from a program of education and training." [3]

Is there a right to education for mentally retarded persons under Federal statute?

Yes. A recent Federal law [4] requires all states receiving Federal aid to their schools to provide an appropriate education for *all* the handicapped children in the state. No child who needs a special program to enable him to have a free public education can be denied that program. The law applies both to handicapped children who are out of school and not receiving educational services and to handicapped children who are enrolled in school but who are not receiving programs and services adequate to meet their needs.

Under this law, states are required to develop plans with the following components: provision of "full educational opportunities" to all; due process safeguards which aid parents in challenging decisions regarding the education of their children; a guarantee that handicapped children will be educated in the mainstream to the fullest possible extent; procedures to assure that tests and other materials used to evaluate a child's special needs are not culturally or racially biased; and a plan to identify and evaluate all children in the state who have special needs.

What are the constitutional theories and the leading judicial decisions supporting a right to education for mentally retarded persons?

While the Constitution does not specifically guarantee citizens a right to education, it does guarantee them both equal protection and due process of the laws. The equal protection provision prohibits the government from unfairly discriminating against an individual or a group of individuals. Therefore, when government undertakes to provide education under compulsory-education laws, it cannot discriminate against a mentally retarded child by excluding or postponing his education, since these children too can learn. Furthermore, due process requires that exclusionary actions taken by government, as well as procedures for processing objections to school exclusions, must be in accord with the fundamental concepts of fairness. The manner in which the equal protection and due process clauses operate to provide the mentally retarded with a right to public education is well illustrated by the two leading right-to-education cases: *Pennsylvania Association for Retarded Children v. Pennsylvania* [5] (the *"PARC"* case) and *Mills v. Board of Education.* [6]

The plaintiffs in the *PARC* case were the Pennsylvania Association for Retarded Children, fourteen named retarded children who were denied an appropriate education at public expense in Pennsylvania and the class of all other children similarly situated. The defendants were the Commonwealth of Pennsylvania, the Secretary of the Department of Education, the State Board of Education, the Secretary of the Department of Public Welfare and school districts and intermediate units in the Commonwealth of Pennsylvania.

After the initial complaint was filed the parties came together and agreed to certain findings and conclusions and to relief to be provided to the named plaintiffs and to the members of their class. A stipulation by the parties, approved and ordered into effect by the court on June 18, 1971, focused on the due process rights of children alleged to be mentally retarded. The court's order specifically states that no such child may be denied admission to a public school program or have his educational status changed without first being accorded notice and the opportunity for a due process hearing. This order outlines due process requirements in detail, beginning with notification of parents that their child is being considered for a change in educational status and ending with detailed provisions for a formal due process hearing, including representation by legal counsel, the right to examine the child's record before the hearing, the right to present evidence of one's own and to cross-examine other witnesses, the right to independent medical, psychological and educational evaluation, the right to a transcribed record of the hearing and the right to a decision on the record.

How does Mills v. Board of Education build upon and expand the holding in the PARC case?

The Mills case was brought as a class action before the Federal District Court in the District of Columbia. Plaintiffs were school-age children, residents of the District of Columbia, who had been denied placement in a publicly supported educational program for substantial periods of time because of alleged mental, behavioral, physical or emotional handicaps or deficiencies. Defendants were the Board of Education and its members, Mayor Walter Washington, the Director of the Social Security Administration and various administrators of the D.C. school system.

Plaintiffs asked the court to declare their rights and to order defendants not to exclude them from the District of Columbia public schools nor to deny them publicly supported education, and to compel the defendants to provide them with immediate and adequate education and facilities in the public schools or alternative placement at public expense.

On August 1, 1972, Judge Joseph C. Waddy's memorandum opinion, judgment and decree were handed down. The court stated that there was no genuine dispute as to the District's responsibilities because Congress had decreed a system of publicly supported education for the children of the District and the Board of Education had been given the responsibiilty for administering this system according to law, including the responsibility for providing education to all "exceptional" children. Although defendants admitted their duty, the court noted that "[t]hroughout these proceedings it has been obvious to the Court that the defendants have no common program or plan for the alleviation of the problems posed by this litigation and that this lack of communication, cooperation and plan is typical and contributes to the problem." [7]

The court found that the plaintiffs were entitled to relief because of applicable statutes and regulations of the District's code and the United States Constitution.

As to the constitutional basis for the holding, Judge Waddy found plaintiffs' right to education was guaranteed by the due process clause of the Fifth Amendment, and cited precedents such as *Brown v. Board of Education*, outlawing school segregation, and *Hobson v. Hansen*,[8] abolishing the so-called track system in the District. The court held that

"the defendants' conduct here, denying plaintiffs and their class not just an equal publicly supported education but all publicly supported education while providing such education to other children, is violative of the Due Process Clause.

"Not only are plaintiffs and their class denied the publicly supported education to which they are entitled, [but] many are suspended or expelled from regular schooling or specialized instruction or reassigned without any prior hearing and are given no periodic review thereafter. Due process of law requires a hearing prior to exclusion, termination [or] classification into a special program." [9]

Do school children alleged to be mentally retarded and subject to placement in special-education classes have a right to review of their classification?

Yes. Some of the leading cases in this area are discussed in the chapter on classification at p. 23 above.

How much progress has been made toward securing a right to education for mentally retarded persons?

Progress in this area has been very impressive. As of this writing, right-to-education suits are pending or have recently been decided in more than half of the states. Faced with the prospect of test-case litigation and a new awareness of the constitutional dimensions, a number of state legislatures have enacted express statutory provisions which guarantee equal educational opportunity to the mentally retarded along with other "exceptional" children. Approximately 70 percent of the states now have mandatory provisions for the education of the handicapped. But having these laws on the books does not guarantee that they will be observed. In the education-rights area, as in other areas, securing a declaration of legal rights is only the first step. Monitoring, muckraking, lobbying, political pressure and continuing judicial intervention must all be used by advocates in order to assure that the rights of the mentally retarded are actually enjoyed.

Do mentally retarded adults who were denied public education as children have a present right to compensatory education?

While this is an issue which is only beginning to be tested, the answer would appear to be yes. In a leading educational-classification and placement case, *Lebanks v. Spears*,[10] the court addressed the issue of whether persons harmed by a previous denial of their right to education had a right to compensatory education. The *Lebanks* court ordered that education and training opportunities be made available to mentally retarded persons "over twenty-one (21) years of age who were not provided educational services when children." [11] The right to compensatory education has also been raised but is yet to be resolved in recent cases in North Dakota and Washington.

Do mentally retarded children confined in institutions also have a right to education?

Yes. This is especially important since in many state institutions the majority of mentally retarded residents do not participate in any type of educational program. Children cannot be deprived of their right to an education because they happen to live in an institution. In fact, to avoid an equal protection violation, the standards governing the operation of educational programs in institutions must be of the same high caliber as those required of public schools within the state system. In the *Wyatt* case, described at p. 57, the Federal court ordered that

> "Residents shall have a right to receive suitable educational services regardless of chronological age, degree of retardation, or accompanying disabilities or handicaps. . . . School-age residents shall be provided with a full and suitable educational program. Such educational program shall meet [proscribed] minimum standards. . . ." [12]

Of course, education of an institutionalized child does not have to take place within the confines of the institution. With transportation, children who reside in institutions may be able to participate in regular or special classes of the local public schools, enabling the child to maintain more normal community ties and enhancing his possibilities for eventual reintegration into society.

What about the claim by school superintendents that there is no money for special education of mentally retarded persons?

The short answer is that an alleged lack of necessary

fiscal resources is not an adequate excuse for the equal protection or due process violations involved in the denial of equal educational opportunity to the mentally retarded. In the *Mills* case, for example, the defendants conceded that they had the legal duty to provide a publicly supported education to each resident of the District of Columbia who is capable of benefiting from such instruction. Their excuse for failing to provide such an education to "exceptional" children was a lack of funds. Judge Waddy's reply to this defense was clear and emphatic:

> "If sufficient funds are not available to finance all of the services and programs that are needed and desirable in the system then the available funds must be expended equitably in such a manner that no child is entirely excluded from a publicly supported education consistent with his needs and ability to benefit therefrom. The inadequacies of the District of Columbia Public School System, whether occasioned by insufficient funding or administrative inefficiency, certainly cannot be permitted to bear more heavily on the 'exceptional' or handicapped child than on the normal child." [13]

NOTES

1. For a definition of "education" as contrasted with "treatment" and "habilitation" see p. 71, note 1.
2. 347 U.S. 483, 493 (1954). *But cf. San Antonio Indep. School Dist. v. Rodriguez*, 411 U.S. 1 (1973).
3. *Pennsylvania Ass'n for Retarded Children v. Pennsylvania*, 334 F. Supp. 1257, 1259 (E.D. Pa. 1971).
4. Education of the Handicapped Amendments of 1974, Pub.L.No. 93-380, §§611-621 (Aug. 21, 1974), *codified at* 20 U.S.C. §§1401 *et seq.* (Supp. IV, 1974). Of particular importance is §615, 20 U.S.C. §1413(b) (Supp. IV, 1974).

5. 334 F. Supp. 1257 (E.D.Pa. 1971).
6. 348 F. Supp. 866 (D.D.C. 1972).
7. *Id.* at 873
8. 269 F.Supp. 401 (D.D.C. 1967).
9. 348 F.Supp 875 (D.D.C. 1972).
10. 60 F.R.D. 135 (E.D.La. 1973) (consent decree).
11. *Id.* at 140.
12. *Wyatt v. Stickney,* 344 F. Supp. 387, 396-97 (M.D.Ala. 1972), *aff'd in part, remanded in part sub nom. Wyatt v. Aderholt,* 503 F.2d. 1305 (5th Cir. 1974).
13. 348 F. Supp. at 876.

THE RIGHT TO LIVE IN THE COMMUNITY

How do zoning regulations discriminate against mentally retarded persons?

Zoning is a systematic regulation of the use and development of real property. Zoning restricts the ways in which an owner can use his property. The exercise of zoning restrictions has traditionally been justified as an adjunct of the government's police power to protect the public safety and welfare. Every state either has legislation or direct constitutional provisions granting to various municipal entities the power to zone for the general welfare. Local units are permitted broad discretion because state statutes generally require only that zoning ordinances prohibit what is harmful to health, morals, safety or welfare, rather than setting out detailed substantive standards.[1]

As discussed at pp. 17-18 above, the normalization principle involves making available to mentally retarded persons patterns and conditions of everyday life which are as close as is practically possible to the norms and patterns of the mainstream of society.[2] In the case of residential services, normalization describes the development of a continuum of models, including family care, foster care, adoption, independent apartment living and small group homes which provide residents with as close to a regular "family" environment as possible. As warehousing institutions come under increasing attack, states are turning to foster or group homes for residential care of the mentally retarded. Such a home will generally house a small group of mentally retarded residents and be licensed by the state according to the number of residents and the types of handicaps which they possess. The operator of a licensed foster or group home for the mentally retarded is usually a private person who owns or leases a house and is paid by the state agency for the room and board provided. Habilitation and training is usually not one of the services provided by the operator or the facility; these services occur off the premises or are provided by a specialist who comes into the home.

Unfortunately, many cities and counties throughout the nation are attempting to prohibit the dispersal of mentally retarded persons in these more normal living situations throughout the community. In most instances, the reaction assumes the form of exclusion of foster or group homes from residential zones. In theory, zoning restricts, for the benefit of the neighborhood as a whole, the ways an owner can use his own property. But zoning can also exclude certain groups of people from residential areas—usually the poor and ethnic minorities, but also the mentally retarded. The issue, then, is how to overcome discriminatory exclusion of family-care homes for mentally retarded persons from residential zones and particularly from "single-family" residential zones.

Why do residential communities object to foster and group homes in their neighborhoods?

Perhaps because of myths (unsupported by evidence) that the mentally retarded possess a high propensity for criminality, that they are over-sexed or that they are carriers of disease. Or perhaps because the neighbors are concerned that a residential normalization program will place disproportionate social costs on their immediate neighborhood—that standards for the site and facility will not assure reasonable privacy to neighbors, that effective neighborhood participation in the management of the facility is not contemplated, or that there is no mechanism which limits the number of "different" facilities in what was intended to be a traditional single-family neighborhood.

Apart from prejudice against mentally retarded persons, the source of opposition may be neighborhoods' concern that if they allow group homes for mentally retarded, then other nontraditional forms of "family" living will follow—boarding houses, rooming houses and halfway houses for alcoholics, drug addicts and sex offenders. The zoning problem may arise from a combination both of prejudice and legitimate neighborhood concerns about bearing only a reasonable part of the social costs of deinstitutionalization.

But if deinstitutionalization is to be successful, effective legal advocacy must be coordinated with good community relations: efforts to communicate with neighbors about the program, practical steps to alleviate their concerns, meaningful guarantees that the residential facility is adequate for the purposes envisioned.

What are the two basic zoning barriers used to exclude group homes from residential areas?

One exclusionary zoning barrier involves ordinances or administrative interpretations expressly excluding group homes for mentally retarded persons from some or all residential zones. Among such ordinances are those which limit some zones to "single family dwellings" and which define "family" narrowly. In a recent case,[3] the plaintiff company contended that the group homes it operated qualified as "single family dwellings" but the defendant zoning board ruled that the homes did not so qualify because the number of residents in such homes exceeded the statutory maximum. Under similar logic, administrative interpretations have also held state-licensed and supported group homes to be a business use of property and have therefore restricted them to nonresidential zones.[4] Other administrative interpretations have defined foster homes for the mentally retarded as a use requiring medical supervision due to the mental condition of the residents and have therefore held that they must be limited to zones where municipal hospitals, nursing homes or convalescent hospitals are allowed.[5]

A second type of exclusionary ordinance contemplates the existence of local variation in the uses permitted in a zone and provides for exceptions or conditional-use permits at the discretion of an administrative body. The granting or withholding of such a permit is often tied to a vague "general welfare" standard or, alternatively, to a "nuisance" standard.

The plaintiffs in one recent suit [6] were given a zoning variance for a group home only after they filed to prevent the defendants—neighbors and city officials—from obstructing the establishment of a group home in a two-family dwelling. The unarticulated premise in such cases is that the application for a conditional-use permit has been denied because of the uneasiness of nearby residents about living in close proximity to mentally retarded persons. The difficulty of appealing the decision of a planning commission or city council is the reluctance of courts to review administrative decisions without a clear showing of abuse of discretion or of fraud.

What are the legal theories which can be used to challenge zoning barriers?

A court could be asked to invalidate an exclusionary zoning ordinance or administrative interpretations of ordinances on the grounds that: (1) the local zoning ordinance or interpretation has been expressly or implicitly pre-empted by state statute; (2) a statutory term has been incorrectly interpreted by the zoning authority so as to exclude group homes for the mentally retarded in residential areas; (3) the exclusionary zoning ordinance or interpretation is beyond municipal authority; or (4) the restrictive zoning ordinance or the pattern of denying variances under the zoning ordinance violates the due process and/or equal protection clauses of the United States Constitution.

First, where state- and county-owned homes are provided to mentally retarded persons, they are likely to be beyond the local zoning power. Even where some homes are not actually owned by the state, state policy may protect them. For example, in a recent case upholding the granting of a special-use permit for the construction of institutional housing over the objections of owners of houses in the neighborhood, the district court observed:

> "Our legislature has established as the policy of this State that mentally retarded . . . persons should not be excluded by municipal zoning ordinances from the benefits of normal residential surroundings."[7]

Where zoning ordinances define a "single-family" specifically, thereby excluding group homes for the mentally retarded from certain residential areas, or where statutory-interpretation or municipal-authority arguments fail, the Constitution may still offer to the mentally retarded protection against zoning barriers.

The due process clause of the Fourteenth Amend-

ment to the U.S. Constitution protects mentally retarded persons against restrictions which are clearly
irrational and arbitrary. However, courts have traditionally placed the burden of proving the invalidity
on the person challenging the ordinance. The factual
record must be very compelling. In *Defoe v. San
Francisco City Planning Commission*,[8] for example, the
zoning administrator had ruled that a group home for
six or fewer mentally retarded children was a use
"which required medical supervision" and that such a
use was impermissible in R-1 and R-1-D (single-family
dwellings) zones of the city. Plaintiffs submitted expert affidavits at trial to document that foster-home
care for mentally retarded children did not require
medical supervision and that the zoning administrator's
ruling was therefore arbitrary, irrational and a denial
of due process.

The traditional equal protection test under the Fourteenth Amendment asks whether a zoning ordinance
and the classification it creates bear a reasonable relation to a legitimate government objective. The most
discriminatory zoning classification that could be made
regarding living arrangements for the mentally retarded would allow nonretarded persons to live in
group settings while denying such an opportunity to
mentally retarded persons. This situation too was presented by *Defoe,* where the City Planning Commission interpreted the code to permit the placement of
nonretarded children in a foster home upon referral
by a responsible public or private social-welfare
agency. But the City Planning Commission allowed
no more than two mentally retarded children in a
licensed group home located in a single-family residential district. Plaintiffs alleged that no legitimate interest of the municipality would be served by
classifying mentally retarded foster children differently
from nonretarded foster children and that such action
was a violation of equal protection.

NOTES

1. This chapter draws heavily upon Chandler & Ross, "Zoning Restrictions and the Right to Live in the Community" and the "reaction comment" by John Deutch in *The Mentally Retarded Citizen and the Law* (M. Kindred et al., eds. 1976). The source of the zoning power—whether a municipal entity zones under charter, home-rule power or the state zoning law —will be an important factor in litigation.

2. Nirje, "A Scandinavian Visitor Looks at U.S. Institutions," in *Changing Patterns in Residential Services for the Mentally Retarded* 51, 181 (R. Kugel & W. Wolfensberger eds. 1969).

3. *Browndale Int'l. Ltd. v. Board of Adjustment*, 60 Wis. 2d 182, 208 N.W. 2d 121 (1973), *cert. denied*, 416 U.S. 936 (1974).

4. *See, e.g., Seaton v. Clifford*, 24 Cal. App. 3d 46, 100 Cal. Rptr. 779 (1972).

5. This was the administrative interpretation challenged by plaintiffs in *Defoe v. San Francisco City Planning Comm'n.*, Civ. No. 30789 (San Francisco, Cal. Super. Ct., filed Aug. 17, 1970).

6. *Doe v. Damm*, Complaint No. 627 (E.D. Mich., filed Mar. 8, 1973).

7. *Anderson v. City of Shoreview*, No. 401575 (2d Judic. Dist., Ramsey County, Minn., June 24, 1975), sl. op. at 41.

8. *Supra*, note 5.

SEXUAL AND MARITAL RIGHTS

Should mentally retarded persons have a right to get married?

Yes. The right to marry is fundamental to all citizens. As the Supreme Court has said:

"The freedom to marry has long been recognized as one of the vital personal rights essential to the orderly pursuit of happiness by free men.

"Marriage is one of the 'basic civil rights of man,' fundamental to our very existence and survival."[1]

Unfortunately, many states consider mentally retarded persons incapable of giving valid consent to a marriage contract on the theory that retardation impairs their capacity to understand and appreciate the meaning and ramifications of the contract. Some states which take this approach explicitly presume that all mentally retarded persons are incompetent to contract for marriage. Other states prohibit the marriage of any person not legally competent to form a binding civil contract, without distinguishing between complicated commercial contracts and such personal arrangements as the marriage contract. Still other states allow a mentally retarded applicant for a marriage license to overcome a presumption against contractual capacity by submitting testimonial evidence of his or her ability to understand a marriage arrangement.

But as has been discussed earlier, there are varying degrees of mental retardation which involve a broad range of abilities and capacities. A single undifferentiated classification of all mentally retarded persons as incompetent to enter into a marriage contract, or even a rebuttable presumption of such incapacity, is therefore recognized by mental-retardation professionals as lacking a rational basis. Such discriminatory laws, based upon inaccurate generalizations and treating mentally retarded persons differently from other persons with respect to the fundamental right to marry, violate the due process and equal protection clauses of the Constitution.

Should mental retardation be grounds for annulment or divorce?

The mental or emotional condition of marriage partners is relevant to the soundness of all marriages. Many states recognize this through laws which generally allow divorce on the grounds of mental instability. But an assumption that mental retardation automatically justifies divorce is just as incorrect as the assumption that it always precludes marriage. Nevertheless, many state laws either allow or compel the dissolution of marital bonds through divorce or annulment on the basis of a spouse's retardation. Since there is no reason to believe that retardation interferes with a marriage any more than other forms of mental and emotional distress, there is no basis for a rule that *compels* separation on the basis of retardation regardless of the desire of the spouses.

Before the answer to this question can be fully understood, the difference between divorce and annulment must be clarified. A divorce is a decree used to dissolve a marriage contract that was previously valid and binding. An annulment is a determination that the marriage never was valid and that the marriage agreement was void at the time it was made. States which have adopted the contract theory in regulating marriage grant an annulment when a marriage partner, by reason of his or her mental condition, lacked the capacity to give legally binding consent at the time of marriage. These states treat the marriage as if it never legally existed. Therefore, any property settlement or transactions based on the marriage have no effect, the inheritance rights derived from a marital relationship do not operate, and no legal obligations regarding post-marital property settlements or support obligations attach, as they would in divorces. Where mentally retarded persons are not prevented from marrying, their mental condition may nevertheless be grounds for divorce. Commitment of a spouse to a mental institution is regarded by some states as sufficient evidence of irretrievable marital breakdown to support a divorce decree.

Can sex education and birth control materials be used by mentally retarded persons who live in the community?

Yes. Any mentally retarded person may voluntarily seek and receive birth control information and material through normal channels. Voluntary methods of birth control are available to noninstitutionalized mentally retarded persons in the same manner they are to nonretarded persons—through purchase and/or prescription. There are no laws that prohibit a private doctor from prescribing birth control for a mentally retarded patient. Educational and instructional material which explain different methods of contraception have been developed specifically for mentally retarded persons. Family-planning and birth control counseling services for mentally retarded persons exist in many communities.

What are the justifications given for involuntary sterilization?

Beginning with Indiana in 1906, states began to pass statutes providing for the compulsory sterilization of individuals referred to as "mentally defective," "idiots" or "imbeciles." Most of these statutes were passed following the United States Supreme Court's endorsement of such laws in *Buck v. Bell*.[2]

Two primary justifications were given for enacting these statutes. Originally sterilization was justified on the eugenic ground that society would be improved if it prevented the reproduction of "inferior individuals" or those who were considered likely to become wards of the state. A newer justification is that mentally retarded persons are incapable of being good parents and should therefore be sterilized.

Despite challenges, the constitutionality of such statutes was generally upheld in the past. In the *Buck* case, which upheld a Virginia sterilization law that was challenged as violating procedural due process and equal protection, Justice Holmes endorsed the right of the state to sterilize those it believed would be a drain on society's resources. In this case, he uttered the now infamous dictum, "Three generations of imbeciles are enough."

Recent empirical studies have, however, brought into question the factual assumptions on which sterilization statutes rest. Geneticists have discovered that the hereditary factors in mental retardation may be so intertwined with other factors, such as birth defects, improper prenatal care and environmental factors, as to make determination of the precise cause of mental retardation almost impossible. Although, some types of mental retardation are demonstrably inherited, studies indicate that between 80 and 90 percent of mentally retarded children are born to apparently normal parents.[3] When only one of the marriage partners is retarded, the chances of normal offspring are 88 percent.[4]

Moreover, it is overgeneralizing to say that retarded people make poor parents. Empirical evidence suggests that mentally retarded persons can sometimes be very good parents. Nor is there any foundation for an overall presumption that mentally retarded parents are unable to provide adequate care for their children: Several studies indicate that I.Q. is irrelevant to childraising ability.[5]

Finally, the evidence refutes another basic assumption used to justify involuntary-sterilization statutes: that mentally retarded persons, unlike "normal" persons, do not suffer from the substantial anxiety reactions and psychological stress which are traditionally associated with sterilization.[6] Given the absence of empirical evidence to support the assumption upon which such statutes rest, it is tragic that twenty-six states still have outmoded laws which permit involuntary sterilization.[7]

Why are statutes which allow involuntary sterilization unconstitutional?

Involuntary-sterilization statutes are unconstitutional because they contemplate intrusion upon mentally retarded persons' constitutionally protected rights to privacy, liberty and procreation, and because such intrusion upon constitutionally protected rights cannot be justified even as rationally related to a legitimate state interest.

The decision to bear a child is within the zone of constitutionally protected individual privacy. In its recent decision striking down a general state-imposed ban on abortions,[8] the Supreme Court relied on the individual's right privately to determine whether to bear a child. Earlier the court had ruled that a Massachusetts statute prohibiting the distribution of contraceptives to unmarried persons was an unconstitutional violation of the right to privacy.[9] "If the right of privacy means anything," wrote the court, "it is the right of the *individual,* married or single, to be free from unwarranted governmental intrusion into matters so fundamentally affecting a person as the decision whether to bear or beget a child." [10] These cases establish that the individual's decision not to have a child lies within the zone of his personal privacy.

The decision to bear a child can also be viewed as an exercise of personal liberty. Indeed, this decision is so basic that it was considered a "fundamental liberty" by several Supreme Court justices.[11] Moreover, scholars view the right to procreate either as an aspect of the right to privacy or the right to liberty, a fundamental right in itself.

Since important and perhaps fundamental rights are infringed by involuntary sterilization, the state must show that it is rationally related to and necessary to the accomplishment of legitimate state goals, and an infringement no greater than necessary to accomplish such goals. As the factual assumptions supporting earlier sterilization laws have been discredited, the justifications for such statutes have properly come under legal attack. Since the state's originally legitimate interests in reducing genetically defective offspring and in promoting parental competence no longer appear to be served by involuntary sterilization of all mentally retarded persons, such laws would appear to be unconstitutional.

Yet another constitutional argument by those who challenge involuntary-sterilization statutes is that such statutes deny mentally retarded persons the equal protection of the laws. The equal protection clause assures that no group of persons will be separated out for disadvantageous regulation by society unless such special regulation can be justified on the basis of differences. While some statutes justify sterilizing mentally retarded persons on the basis of unscientific predictions that they might not be good parents, the same statutes do *not* require sterilization for "normal" parents, even when there is an actual history of child abuse. Further, no state would allow sterilization of a "normal" person even if there were a 90-percent chance of a serious birth defect. Nevertheless some states attempt to justify sterilization of mentally retarded persons where the likelihood of their bearing a retarded child is far smaller. Since there is no rational basis of singling out mentally retarded persons for sterilization, such laws violate the right to equal protection on their face. These same statutes are often attacked as being *applied* in a discriminatory fashion, in that their actual effect—if not their intent—is to permit specific disfavored groups, such as blacks or unwed mothers, to be labeled mentally retarded and then sterilized, while others retain their basic right to procreate without interference by the state.

Involuntary sterilization may also run afoul of the constitutional principle which requires that limitations upon important liberties be no more restrictive than necessary to accomplish legitimate state goals. Even if in some instances a legitimate state interest can be found which justifies limiting procreation by certain mentally retarded persons, then other less drastic forms of contraception must be used, provided they are likely to be effective.

Finally, in those limited situations where the state does argue that it can establish a legitimate interest in the sterilizing of a particular mentally retarded person, procedural due process requires that the subject of this proposed sterilization have notice, a hearing and other basic protections, such as the right to counsel, the right to cross-examine opposing witnesses and to present witnesses of his or her own before the decision to sterilize becomes final. If such safeguards are not provided, a violation of procedural due process will have taken place.

A recent decision by a three-judge district court in Alabama shows how traditional state involuntary-sterilization statutes are likely to be re-examined and struck down. The statute in Alabama authorized sterilization of residents of Partlow State School at the discretion of the Superintendent of Mental Health and his assistant. It contained no provision for a hearing at which the prospective patient could protest the action, no requirement of prior notice and no right of the subject to legal representation or to appeal the decision to the courts. On December 20, 1973, a three-judge panel in *Wyatt v. Aderholt* declared the sterilization statute patently unconstitutional, pointing initially to the absence of provisions for notice and hearing and noting more generally that "[t]he sterilization *vel non* of mentally retarded inmates cannot be left to the unfettered discretion of any two officials or individuals." [12]

May mentally retarded persons be sterilized voluntarily?

If a mentally retarded person's request for sterilization is truly informed, competent and voluntary, it should be honored. But even assuming that full information about the nature of the procedure and alternatives has been given and that the person to be sterilized is able to understand the issue involved and to make a decision, "voluntariness" may be very difficult to assess. One important study found that in "States with a 'voluntary' [sterilization] statute, 'consent' is often more theoretical than real. For example, it may be made a condition of discharge from an institution that the patient 'consent' to sterilization. And in one State our field investigators observed a 'voluntary' sterilization proceeding for a 6-year-old boy." [13]

While the coercive factors which might motivate a mentally retarded person to give a legally invalid "consent" to sterilization are perhaps greatest in total institutions, they can operate in the community as well. Litigation has recently led to special safeguards which attempt to protect mentally retarded persons from subtle and no-so-subtle pressures to consent to sterilization, both within institutions [14] and at Federally funded family-planning programs in the community. [15]

In Alabama, after the three-judge court had declared Alabama's compulsory-sterilization statute unconstitutional, the Federal District Court hearing the *Wyatt* case issued a detailed order containing substantive and procedural standards governing "voluntary sterilization." This order established *inter alia* that sterilization must be in the "best interest" of the individual and may not be undertaken for "institutional convenience;" that no one under 21 may be sterilized except as a "medical necessity;" that written consent must be obtained from competent persons requesting sterilization; that residents must be provided the opportunity to consult with counsel before opting for sterilization; and that no coercion shall be used to encourage institutional residents to volunteer for this procedure.

Traditionally, sterilization of a retarded person with

the consent of a guardian or next of kin has been regarded as "voluntary." But as long as the person primarily affected is able to express an opinion on the sterilization, there is no arguable basis for relying on the consent of someone else—especially given growing recognition that the interests of parents or guardians and their mentally retarded children or wards are not always the same. (See pp. 36 to 38.) Moreover, even when the mentally retarded person subject to sterilization is not competent to make a decision for himself, there is a growing trend to provide extra protections to assure that the decision to sterilize is in his best interest. In one recent case, for example, a juvenile court authorized sterilization of a mentally retarded female child whose mother had petitioned the court for approval. The appellate court reversed, holding that the juvenile court lacked jurisdiction to deny the daughter the fundamental right to bear a child.[16] And in another recent case, the father of a mentally retarded 19-year-old woman, who was also her temporary guardian, petitioned the court for an order authorizing him to consent to her sterilization. A separate guardian *ad litem* made an oral report to the court in opposition to the petition, and the court denied the petition to consent to sterilization on the grounds that where the evidence that sterilization was in the best interest of the ward was in dispute, any doubts should be resolved against sterilization.[17]

Can an abortion legally be performed on a mentally retarded woman against her will?

Involuntary abortions are unconstitutional for the same reasons that involuntary sterilizations are unconstitutional. (See discussion at pp. 115-119.)

Many states have statutes authorizing the superintendents of institutions to permit "emergency" operations on institutional residents, and these statutes might be used to justify involuntary abortions in the case of genuine medical emergency. But there have been charges that some hospital administrators perform abortions on retarded residents without the subject's consent even when the situation is not an emergency. Since abortions can be considered surgical procedures, state law regarding the authority of administrators to perform nonemergency operations without the consent of the resident or guardian should be consulted. Unauthorized abortions might constitute both a violation of laws regulating nonemergency surgery and the tort of assault and battery.

May a mentally retarded parent be denied custody of his child because of his mental condition?

The competence of mentally retarded persons to act as parents, like their capacity for any other activity, should be determined on an individual basis. There is no justification for automatically assuming that a mentally retarded person will be an inadequate parent; in fact, some studies disclose a negative correlation between I.Q. and parental competence.[18] Furthermore, custody laws based on the presumed incompetence of mentally retarded parents violate equal protection because they establish an arbitrary classification. Many inadequate parents who seriously abuse their children are considered normal on the basis of intellectual level and social or professional status, even though they perform as less competent parents than many mentally retarded persons. Although we lack adequate predictive tools to distinguish beforehand between suitable and unsuitable parents, the absence of such refined techniques does not justify discriminating against mentally retarded parents in custody matters.

Nevertheless, such incorrect and overbroad assumptions serve as a basis for laws in many states which restrict the child-rearing rights of mentally retarded persons. While no state permanently denies a parent custody of his child without a hearing on his parental competence or the child's welfare, some states regard the parent's commitment to a mental institution—past as well as present—as sufficient evidence to authorize the child's removal and adoption. In light of the established Supreme Court precedent that child-rearing is a fundamental liberty protected by the Fourteenth Amendment,[19] such laws restricting the parental rights of mentally retarded persons are open to serious challenge.

NOTES

1. *Loving v. Virginia,* 388 U.S. 1, 12 (1967).
2. 274 U.S. 200 (1927).
3. *The Mentally Disabled and the Law* 212 (S. Brakel & R. Rock eds. 1971).
4. Roos, "Psychological Impact of Sterilization on the Individual," 1 *Law & Psychology Rev.* 45, 47 (1975).
5. *Id.*
6. *Id.* at 50-51.
7. Steinbock *et al.,* "Civil Rights of the Mentally Retarded: An Overview," 1 *Law & Psychology Rev.* 151, 175 (1975).
8. *Roe v. Wade,* 410 U.S. 113 (1973).
9. *Eisenstadt v. Baird,* 405 U.S. 438 (1972).
10. *Id.* at 453 (emphasis in original).
11. *Griswold v. Connecticut,* 381 U.S. 479, 495-99 (1965) (Goldberg, J., concurring, joined by Warren, C.J. & Brennan, J.).
12. *Wyatt v. Aderholt,* 368 F. Supp. 1382, 1383 (M.D. Ala. 1973).
13. R. Allen, *Legal Rights of the Disabled and Disadvantaged* 20 (1969).
14. *Wyatt v. Aderholt, supra* note 12.
15. *Relf v. Weinberger,* 372 F. Supp. 1196 (D.D.C. 1974), *remanded for supplementation,* Nos. 74-1798, 74-1802 (D.C. Cir., Apr. 18, 1975), *on remand,* 403 F. Supp. 1235 (1975), *appeal pending.*
16. *In re MKR,* 515 S.W. 2d 467 (Mo. 1974).

17. *In re Mary Louise Anderson* (Dane County Court, Branch I, Wis., Nov. 1974).
18. Roos, *supra* note 4, at 47.
19. *See* cases cited at notes 1, 8-11, *supra*.

THE RIGHT TO A BARRIER-FREE ENVIRONMENT

Is it true that many mentally retarded persons also have physical handicaps?

Yes. According to a recent study, almost 95 percent of those with an I.Q. below 30 and almost 78 percent of those with an I.Q. between 30 and 55 suffer from at least one major physically handicapping condition.[1] Among the mildly mentally retarded, this percentage declines to 37 percent.[2] It is estimated that over 30 percent of *all* mentally retarded children suffer from additional physical handicaps and that this proportion increases with age and with greater severity of retardation.[3]

Do mentally retarded persons with physical handicaps have a right to public facilities which are accessible to them?

Yes. Historically, public policies have ignored the needs of persons with physical handicaps in the construction of public facilities. Recently, however, statutory and constitutional theories have been used in successful challenges to "architectural barriers." Also, legislatures have passed a number of laws to help eliminate architectural barriers. The Architectural Barriers Act of 1968, as amended,[4] provides that any structure built by the Federal government for its own use or financed in whole or in part by Federal funds (except for private residences) must meet Federal standards to insure its accessiblity to persons who are physically handicapped. Many states have also passed legislation to eliminate architectural barriers in public buildings. As of August 1973, every state except Kentucky had some legislation regarding architectural barriers.[5]

In addition to lawsuits stemming directly from state and federal statutory provisions, a number of constitutional theories have been raised by advocates attacking architectural barriers on behalf of the mentally retarded.

First, where the government conducts public functions it may not unreasonably discriminate against mentally or physically handicapped persons. Therefore public policies which permit architectural barriers may violate the equal protection clause of the Fourteenth Amendment to the United States Constitution. A variant of the equal protection argument is that physically handicapped persons are denied equal employment opportunity if they are denied government jobs because public buildings are physically inaccessible to them.

Other theories are that architectural barriers which prevent physically handicapped persons from using public transportation violate their First Amendment right to travel; that physically handicapped persons' First Amendment right to petititon the government is denied when government officials are inaccessible because of architectural barriers in public buildings; and that physically handicapped persons are denied equal access to the courts when they cannot enter the courthouse because of architectural barriers.

What kinds of remedies have been won in architectural-barrier cases?

Plaintiffs in architectural-barrier cases generally seek orders requiring that architectural barriers be removed from existing facilities and that future facilities be designed in a "barrier-free" manner. In one recent case, for example, a physically handicapped law student confined to a wheelchair filed suit after he had tried unsuccessfully to enter various county buildings which were designed in such a way as to be inaccessible to persons in wheelchairs.[6] This case was settled with a consent decree. The county defendants agreed to install ramps, a bell or signaling device or other appropriate means to enable physically handicapped persons to use certain public buildings.

In another recent case,[7] a Federal court ordered the Washington D.C. local transit authority not to use stations in its new subway system until they are made accessible to physically handicapped persons.

An issue likely to be litigated in the near future is the right of mentally retarded persons with physical handicaps to airline travel. A number of the airlines refuse to fly physically disabled persons.

Must architects and planners allow for any other special handicaps of mentally retarded persons?

Yes. For example, mass-transit systems may be unusable by mentally retarded persons who cannot read or count the change necessary to pay the fare. The challenge in design of such systems is to minimize all barriers to their use by mentally retarded persons.

NOTES

1. R. Conley, *The Economics of Mental Retardation* 47 (1973).
2. *Id.*
3. *Id.* at 48.
4. 42 U.S.C. §§4151-4156 (1970).
5. President's Committee on Employment of the Handicapped, *Survey of State Laws to Remove Barriers*

(Available from PCEH, 1111-20th Street, N.W., Washington, D.C. 20036).

6. *Friedman v. County of Cuyahoga,* Case No. 895961 (Cuyahoga County, Ohio C.P., Nov. 15, 1972) (consent decree).

7. *Urban League v. WMATA,* Civil No. 776-72 (D.D.C., Plaintiffs' Motion for Summary Judgment granted, Oct. 9, order issued Oct. 24, 1973).

EMPLOYMENT RIGHTS

What rights do mentally retarded persons have to employment in the community?

Mentally retarded persons are subjected, like other minority groups, to various forms of job discrimination. A major step in dealing with this problem was passage of the Rehabilitation Act of 1973.[1] The Act grants a statutory right to the handicapped to be free from employment discrimination and requires certain employers to take affirmative action to employ qualified handicapped persons. Regulations to assure compliance with Section 503 of the Act, which requires government contractors to take affirmative action to employ and advance in employment qualified handicapped individuals, have now been promulgated by the Secretary of Labor.[2]

Can mentally retarded persons perform some kinds of work as well or better than other workers?

It is now generally accepted that mentally retarded workers are particularly well suited for, and perform *better* than nonretarded workers, certain kinds of important but highly repetitive tasks.[3] Once properly placed, mentally retarded workers have proven more reliable than nonretarded employees. For example, a study by the U.S. Civil Service Commission of 7,442 mentally retarded individuals who were appointed to positions in forty federal agencies located in every state showed that the turnover rate for these mentally retarded employees "compares favorably with turnover rates for all employees in similar grades."[4]

NOTES

1. 29 U.S.C. §§701 *et seq., as amended* (Supp IV, 1974).
2. 20 C.F.R. §§741.1 *et seq.* (1975).
3. *See, e.g.,* President's Committee on Mental Retardation, MR71: *Entering the Era of Human Ecology* 27 (1971); President's Committee on Employment of the Handicapped and the National Association for Retarded Children, *About Jobs and Mentally Retarded People* 2, 17, 18 (1972); President's Panel on Mental Retardation, *Report of the Task Force on Law* 5-7 (1963).
4. U.S. Civil Service Commission, *An 8½ Year Record: Mentally Retarded Workers in the Federal Service* 2 (Nov. 1972).

THE RIGHT TO BE FREE FROM DISCRIMINATION IN VOTING, DRIVING AND EXERCISING OTHER BASIC RIGHTS AND PRIVILEGES OF CITIZENSHIP.

Do mentally retarded persons have the right to be free from discrimination in voting, driving and exercising other basic rights and privileges of citizens?

Yes. Mentally retarded citizens should have the same presumptive right to vote, to drive and to exercise other basic rights and privileges as all other citizens. A flat prohibition of the right to vote or drive would violate the due process and equal protection clauses of the Constitution for the same reasons that a blanket prohibition on education or marriage would violate these same constitutional provisions. (See discussions earlier in this chapter.) Again, the denial of any of these basic rights or privileges can only be justified if it is rationally related to an *individual* inability to exercise the right or privilege.

In the voting area, for example, a group of adult mentally retarded residents of a state school in New Jersey recently sued the clerk of their county Board of Elections claiming that they were denied their right to vote, in violation of the Constitution and statutes of both the United States and New Jersey. The denial was based solely on their status as residents of the school even though each of them had been determined competent to vote by qualified representatives of the Department of Institutions and Agencies.[1] The Superior Court held that the refusal of the clerk to register the plaintiffs was unlawful. Subsequently all of the residents registered to vote and many voted in the next election. In a similar situation, the Supreme Judicial Court of Massachusetts recently struck down a town's attempt to declare the residents of a state school for the mentally retarded as being under the guardianship of the state and, therefore, ineligible to vote.[2] Since many mentally retarded residents of state institutions are finally having their right to vote recognized, the claim of the right to vote is all the more compelling for other mentally retarded persons now living and functioning in the community.

What Federal statute gives mentally retarded persons a general right to be free from discrimination?

Section 504 of the Rehabilitation Act of 1973 provides that:

"No otherwise qualified handicapped indivi-

dual in the United States . . . shall, solely by
reason of his handicap, be excluded from the participation in, be denied the benefits of, or be
subjected to discrimination under any program
or activity receiving Federal financial assistance." [3]

While this section has yet to be tested in litigation—
and there are as yet no regulations clarifying it—section 504 would appear to establish a private Federal
cause of action for discrimination against mentally retarded persons in any programs receiving Federal support.[4]

NOTES

1. *Carroll v. Cobb*, Civil Action No. L-6585-74-P.W.
   (Burlington County, N.J. Super. Ct., Nov. 1974),
   affirmed ———.
2. *Boyd v. Board of Registrars of Voters*, 334 N.E. 2d
   629 (Mass. 1975).
3. 29 U.S.C. §794 (Supp. IV, 1974). For Committee and
   Conference reports on §504 *see* 2 U.S. Code Cong. &
   Admin. News, 93d Cong., 1st Sess. 2076, 2123, 2145,
   2154. Section 504 does not carry express authority or
   direction to any agency to issue regulations for its
   implementation. The HEW Office of Civil Rights has
   been preparing such regulations, but progress has been
   painfully slow and they have not been issued as of
   this writing.
4. *See, e.g.*, Gilhool, "The Right to Community Services,"
   in *The Mentally Retarded Citizen and the Law* (M.
   Kindred et al. eds. 1976).

THE RIGHT TO MEDICAL CARE

Do mentally retarded children with serious physical handicaps have a legal right to medical care?

History tells us that the Spartans would leave weak or damaged children in the wilderness to die. But values change, and several courts have recently recognized a right to life on behalf of seriously handicapped children. In one decision the court ordered surgery to be performed to correct a blocked esophagus after the child's parents had refused to consent to such corrective surgery on the grounds that their child had multiple serious physical handicaps at birth. The court held that "the most basic right enjoyed by every human being is the right to life itself," and that "the doctor's qualitative evaluation of the value of the life to be preserved is not legally within the scope of his expertise."[1] In a similar case, a New Jersey court held that the refusal of parents to authorize a lifesaving operation to correct an intestinal blockage in their child justified a protective-services order making the child a ward of the court for purposes of authorizing the operation.[2]

NOTES

1. *Maine Medical Center v. Houle,* Civil Action No. 74-145 (Cumberland, Me. Super. Ct., Feb. 14, 1974), *reported in* President's Committee on Mental Retardation, Legal Rights Work Group, *Compendium of Law Suits Establishing The Legal Rights of Mentally Retarded Citizens* 66 (Oct. 1974).
2. *In re Babygirl Obernauer,* order relating to protective services (Morris County, N.J. Juv. & Dom. Rel. Ct., Dec. 22, 1970), *reported in* President's Committee on Mental Retardation, Legal Rights Work Group, *Com-*

pendium of Law Suits Establishing The Legal Rights of Mentally Retarded Citizens 67 (Oct. 1974).

RIGHTS UNDER FEDERAL FINANCIAL-ASSISTANCE AND BENEFIT PROGRAMS

What Federal financial-assistance and benefit programs are available for mentally retarded persons?

Major Federal benefit programs include:

Social Security Disability Insurance: [1] A mentally retarded person is eligible for disability insurance if he is severely disabled and has worked a sufficient number of quarters to be covered under Social Security or if he is severely disabled and the child of a covered worker who has retired or is deceased.

Eligible beneficiaries under the disability-insurance program will receive monthly cash benefits so long as the disabling condition exists. Disability-insurance beneficiaries are also eligible for Medicare coverage after a two-year waiting period.

Supplemental Security Income (SSI): [2] Supplemental Security Income is a Federal program for aged, blind and disabled persons with little or no income or assets. Persons eligible under this program can receive monthly cash benefits up to a Federally established monthly ceiling. To become eligible for this program, a mentally retarded person must demonstrate that his combined earned and unearned income and resources are minimal and that his mental retardation alone or in combination with other impairments is of such a severity as to prevent him from earning substantial wages.

Aid to Families with Dependent Children

(AFDC): [8] This program provides monthly cash benefits to families with dependent children in which one parent is absent from the home or, in some cases, present but unable to work. Unlike the SSI program, AFDC is administered by the states and eligibility rules vary considerably across the country. Generally speaking, however, eligibility is based on membership in a family with dependent children whose income is minimal or nonexistent. Some mentally retarded children will be eligible for both SSI and AFDC. In this circumstance, it is generally more advantageous (as well as less stigmatizing) to apply for SSI benefits. Social Security district offices are required to assist SSI applicants in determining which program will provide the largest benefit.

Medicare Program: [4] The Medicare program is a Federal health-insurance program for aged persons and for disabled persons receiving Social Security disability benefits. In the latter case, persons must have received disability benefits for two years before they become eligible for Medicare coverage. Benefits covered by the Medicare program are equivalent to those covered by typical private health-insurance programs and include both hospitalization and outpatient benefits.

Medicaid: [5] The Medicaid program, which is administered by the states, is a program designed to pay the costs of health care for low-income persons. While eligibility rules vary widely from state to state, SSI recipients and AFDC recipients are generally eligible. Covered health services also vary widely from state to state, but at a minimum cover hospitalization, physicians' services, lab tests, developmental screening and skilled nursing services. In many states, Medicaid will also pay the cost of institutional care for mentally retarded persons living in intermediate-care facilities.

CHAMPUS: [6] This is the health program run by the Department of Defense for military personnel and their dependents. It includes a broad spectrum of health care, inpatient and outpatient. In addition, CHAMPUS provides certain special benefits related to rehabilitation, institutional care and community services for mentally and physically handicapped dependents. These special benefits apply primarily to dependents of active-duty personnel and are discontinued within one year after the parent leaves active duty. However, for a child of a member who is killed in action, payments may continue until the child reaches 21.

Survivors of a veteran who has died as the result of a service-connected disability who are not eligible for CHAMPUS and who are under 65 are now eligible for CHAMPVA: *Civilian Health and Medical Program—Veterans Administration.*[7]

For more information on Social Security Disability Insurance, SSI and Medicare, readers should contact their local Social Security offices. For more information on AFDC and Medicaid, readers should contact their local public welfare offices.

In addition to the "personal entitlement" programs described above, there are a wide variety of Federally funded programs which support services for mentally retarded persons. Two of the most important of these programs are:

The Vocational Rehabilitation Program: [8] This program is administered in each state by a state Department of Vocational Rehabilitation. It provides rehabilitative services to disabled persons, including mentally retarded people, as long as they are judged to have "employment potential." Persons are eligible regardless of income.

Social Services: [9] Each of the states administers social services programs with Federal funds provided through Title XX of the Social Security Act. States have great leeway in determining which services to support with their Title XX money. Many states fund programs for mentally retarded persons under this program. Typical examples of Title XX services for mentally retarded people include day care for adults, work-activities centers, recreation programs, transportation programs, etc. Eligibility for these programs is limited to low-income persons, including SSI and AFDC recipients. For local information on these service programs readers should contact either their state Association for Retarded Citizens or their state Developmental Disabilities Council or mental-retardation agency.

More detailed information on both personal-entitlement and benefit programs is available in *How to Provide for Their Future* and the *Social Security Handbook,* cited in the bibliography of this book.

NOTES

1. *See* 42 U.S.C. §§402(d), 416(i), 423, *as amended,* (Supp. IV, 1974).
2. *Id.* §§1381-85, *as amended,* (Supp. IV, 1974).
3. *Id.* §§601 *et seq., as amended,* (Supp. IV, 1974).
4. *Id.* §§1395 *et seq., as amended,* (Supp. IV, 1974).
5. *Id.* §§1396 *et seq., as amended,* (Supp. IV, 1974).
6. 10 U.S.C. §§1071 *et seq.* (1970).
7. 38 U.S.C. §613 (Supp. IV, 1974).
8. *See* 29 U.S.C. §721 (Supp. IV, 1974).
9. 42 U.S.C. §§1397 *et seq.* (Supp. IV, 1974).

V

Rights of Mentally Retarded
Persons in the Criminal Process

**Are mentally retarded persons more likely to commit
criminal acts than other people?**

No. There is no firm evidence to support this contention. However, mentally retarded persons are
disproportionately represented in our country's prison
population. One often-cited study found that, nation-
wide, 9.5 percent of the prison population is mentally
retarded [1]—more than three times the proportion of
mentally retarded persons in the general population.
This 9.5-percent figure fluctuates substantially from
region to region. For instance, almost 25 percent of
the prisoners in Kentucky, Tennessee, Alabama and
Mississippi are classified as mentally retarded.

It should be noted, however, that a high percentage
of prisoners labeled mentally retarded come from economically deprived, culturally disadvantaged groups.
Courts in a number of jurisdictions have questioned
whether the tests used to measure mental retardation
may not be culturally or racially biased. Even assuming the testing instruments are valid, mentally retarded
persons who commit criminal acts are more easily ap-
prehended, more prone to confess, more likely to be
convicted and will probably be incarcerated longer than

nonretarded offenders.[2] Moreover, it may well be that both mental retardation and crime are symptoms of socioeconomic factors rather than causally related to each other.[3]

What special problems are faced by mentally retarded persons in the criminal process?

The most serious special problem faced by mentally retarded persons in the criminal process is the lack of knowledge about and sensitivity to the problems of mental retardation by police, lawyers and judges and their inability to identify accused criminals who are mentally retarded. Failure to identify mental retardation in an accused criminal means that a number of important legal issues which must be raised by a defendant go unconsidered. As will be discussed briefly below, mental retardation is an important factor which must be weighed in determination of competency to stand trial, the admissibility of confessions and criminal responsibility (the insanity defense).

How is mental retardation relevant in decisions regarding the admissibility of confessions?

It is an established principle of American law that a coerced confession cannot be used in evidence against a person accused of crime. Conviction on the basis of a coerced confession not only offends our concept of justice; it may also result in the conviction of innocent persons, since confessions under duress are notoriously untrustworthy.

Among the factors weighed in deciding when the circumstances of a confession render it involuntary are the length of the interrogation, the use of physical brutality or techniques of psychological coercion and the length of time between arrest and arraignment before a magistrate. In holding confessions involuntary —and hence inadmissible in evidence—the Supreme Court has recognized mental retardation as a factor diminishing the ability of an accused person to resist police pressure.[4] This concern is certainly warranted, for, as noted by the Task Force on Law of the President's Panel on Mental Retardation, a mentally retarded person, even when not coerced in the usual sense, may be unable to understand police procedures and their consequences; he may therefore be unable to make a genuine decision in relation to them.[5] The mentally retarded accused criminal is more likely than the nonretarded person to be unaware of his constitutional right to refuse to answer police questions and of his right to consult with an attorney. Even where the interrogator advises him of these rights he may be unable to appreciate their significance. Because of his mental retardation, he is particularly vulnerable both to an atmosphere of threats and to one of friendliness designed by police to induce cooperation.

These issues were addressed by the Massachusetts Supreme Judicial Court in its recent decision in *Commonwealth v. Daniels.*[6] In *Daniels,* the defendant was a mentally retarded young man with a second-grade reading ability and an I.Q. of 53. He was found guilty of murder in the second degree solely on the basis of his confession to the Springfield police. The trial judge filed a memorandum finding that Daniels "did knowingly, willingly, voluntarily, and intelligently waive his constitutional rights under the Miranda warnings," in an act "which was a product of a rational intellect." In reviewing the admissibility of Daniels' confession, the Supreme Judicial Court agreed that an adult with a diminished or subnormal mental capacity may make an effective waiver of his rights and render a voluntary, knowing and admissible confession. The court noted further, however, that "circumstances and techniques of custodial interrogation which pass constitutional muster when applied to a normal adult may not be constitutionally tolerable as applied to one who is immature or mentally deficient." According to the court:

> "The fact that Daniels was mildly to moderately mentally retarded, with an I.Q. of fifty-three, does not compel a determination as a matter of law on this record that Daniels did not knowingly and willingly waive his *Miranda* rights and make a voluntary confession, admissible pursuant to constitutional standards.
>
> * * *
>
> "We have arrived at our view that there should be a new trial because no evidence was presented at the voir dire or at the trial to aid the trier of fact in evaluating the impact of custodial interrogation on Daniels in these circumstances. He might be more suggestible and subject to intimidation than a person of normal intelligence. He might not be able to understand the consequences of his right to a lawyer or his right to remain silent. He might be inclined to state that he understands even when he does not. Many of Daniels' statements that he understood his rights were simple 'yes's' or 'yeah's,' and not reassuring explanations of his asserted comprehension. . . . We do not know enough about intelligence quotients (I.Q.) and mental retardation to rule conclusively on this question. Yet we do know enough to believe the matter needs further analysis."

Given the many factors relating to mental retardation which make confessions by mentally retarded persons questionable, it was suggested by the Task Force on Law of the President's Panel on Mental Retardation that it should be considered improper to question anyone who may be mentally retarded unless his attorney, parent or guardian is present.[7]

Can a mentally retarded defendant enter a valid guilty plea?

Considerations relating to guilty pleas are very similar to those raised by confessions. In a recent decision concerning guilty pleas,[8] a Federal appellate court noted the "basic failure of our criminal justice system to recognize that special provisions must sometimes be made for the mentally retarded." [9] In *United States v. Masthers,* the United States Court of Appeals for the District of Columbia overruled a trial court's denial without a hearing of an allegedly mentally retarded criminal defendant's motions to vacate and withdraw his guilty plea to charges stemming from robbery of a gas station.

Observing that a defendant who enters a guilty plea waives his privilege against cumpulsory self-incrimination, his right to trial by jury and his right to confront his accusers, the court held that if a plea is not both voluntary and competent, it has been obtained in violation of due process and is therefore void.

Although there were early signs suggesting mental retardation, Johnny Masthers was first tested *after* he pleaded guilty. His lawyer informed the court that only upon learning of Masthers' low I.Q.—from a presentence report and an evaluation of his suitability for rehabilitation under the Narcotics Addict Rehabilitation Act—did he appreciate the meaning of earlier signs and realize that his client might have been incompetent to enter a guilty plea. The trial court denied Masthers' motions to vacate his guilty plea based upon:

(1) Masthers' failure to raise the competence issue prior to sentencing;
(2) the court's personal observation of Masthers and the apparent understanding he displayed at the time he gave his guilty plea;
(3) Masthers' admissions of his role in the robbery.

The appellate court found that the relevant Federal statutes and rules of criminal procedure specifically provide for withdrawal of a guilty plea after both conviction and sentencing; that the court's personal observation of Johnny Masthers and opinion that he was competent was an insufficient basis for denying him a hearing on this issue; and that Masthers was entitled to an evidentiary hearing on his competence to plead guilty, regardless of his guilt or innocence. Noting that the interest of Masthers and the administration of criminal justice would best be served by a hearing to properly examine and assess the nature and extent of his disabilities, the appeals court remanded the case to the trial court. As a concurring member of the three-judge panel wrote,

> "We make special effort and provisions to the end that the deaf litigant or the litigant whose comprehension of the English language is poor shall understand what is transpiring in court and act knowingly. It seems neither fair nor humane to refuse to make an analogous appropriate special effort when it appears that an accused person's comprehension is substantially impaired because of mental retardation." [10]

What are the rights of a mentally retarded person who is incompetent to stand trial?

The law does not proceed against a criminal defendant who is not able to understand the nature and object of the proceedings against him or to make a rational defense. Ordinarily, where mentally handicapped persons are found incompetent to stand trial, they are committed to civil facilities with the understanding that a trial will take place after their "recovery." Unlike the mentally ill, however, mentally retarded persons who are found incompetent to stand trial and committed to civil institutions will probably remain incompetent. This precise situation—involving an accused mentally retarded defendant who was incompetent to stand trial and who nearly disappeared in the crack between the civil commitment and criminal commitment systems—was the focus of the Supreme Court's historic decision in *Jackson v. Indiana*.[11] The petitioner in Jackson was a 27-year-old deaf-mute with the mental age of a preschool child and no communicative ability other than through limited sign language. He had been charged with two counts of larceny—essentially purse snatching which involved property worth $9—and was committed to the Indiana Department of Mental Health as incompetent to stand trial. Even though the maximum sentence for these misdemeanors if he had been convicted would have been six months, he had already been involuntarily confined in Indiana Mental Hospital for almost three years and might well have remained there for the rest of his life when his case was heard by the Supreme Court. The Supreme Court decided that:

" . . a person charged by a State with a criminal offense who is committed solely on account of his incapacity to proceed to trial cannot be held more than the reasonable period of time necessary to determine whether there is a substantial probability that he will attain that capacity in the foreseeable future. If it is determined that this is not the case, then the State must either institute the customary civil commitment proceeding that would be required to commit indefinitely any other citizen, or release the defendant. Furthermore, even if it is determined that the defendant probably soon will be able to stand trial, his continued commitment must be justified by progress toward that goal." [12]

If a mentally retarded person is found incompetent

to stand trial, the principle of the least restrictive alternative suggests that he should not automatically be sent to an institution for the so-called "criminal insane" or to a school for the mentally retarded. Rather, the nature and degree of protective care should depend in part on the degree to which the accused person endangers society. The type of care required might range from full custody to a normal life at home, with parents or guardians admonished about the need for closer supervision.

Because the prospect is relatively slim for restoring mentally retarded persons to competency to stand trial and because the stigma of having been charged with a crime can be very severe, it is therefore important to develop alternatives to trials for retarded persons who are likely to be found incompetent. In this regard, the American Law Institute's Model Penal Code calls for a post-commitment hearing—with the possibility that the court may dismiss the charges—in cases where, based on facts or law, counsel for the defendants can demonstrate a defense other than mental disease or defect.[13]

Can mentally retarded defendants assert the insanity defense?

Yes. Although the standard for insanity varies among jurisdictions, the most generally accepted test is that recommended by the American Law Institute: "A person is not responsible for criminal conduct if at the time of such conduct as a result of mental disease or defect he lacks substantial capacity either to appreciate the criminality [wrongfulness] of his conduct or to conform his conduct to the requirement of law." [14] Where the insanity defense is asserted by a mentally retarded person, the jury should consider testimony as to the development, adaptation and functioning of mental or emotional processes and behavior controls.

In *United States v. Brawner*,[15] the United States

Court of Appeals for the District of Columbia adopted this test of criminal responsibility, which also includes the rule of "diminished responsibility" under which mental impairment, though insufficient to exonerate, may nevertheless serve to reduce the degree of the offense. The court held: "Our rule permits the introduction of expert testimony as to abnormal condition if it is relevant to negative, or establish, the specific mental condition that is an element of the crime." [16] Obviously, this new rule affords a basis for introducing evidence of mental retardation to show that the defendant, by virtue of his mental retardation, lacks the specific mental intent that is an element of the crime.

Do mentally retarded persons in the criminal process receive meaningful habilitation?

No. Unfortunately, institutional programs and facilities especially designed for the mentally retarded offender are virtually nonexistent.[17] The care and treatment of mentally retarded offenders is one of the most consistently frustrating problems that confronts administrators of both correctional institutions and residential facilities for the mentally retarded. Mentally retarded offenders are the minority group and misfits in both settings.[18]

Do mentally retarded offenders in prisons have a right to meaningful habilitation programs?

Yes—at least in the opinion of the Task Force on Law of the President's Panel on Mental Retardation, which has observed that punishing mentally retarded offenders by imprisonment should be regarded as repugnant, particularly since it overlooks their special habilitation and educational needs: "[O]nce it has been determined that an offender is mentally retarded to a degree and in a manner making it reasonable to believe his affliction caused the conduct in question, then we think it axiomatic that he should be treated according to his condition. . . . The mentally retarded offender, whether dangerous or not, requires rehabilitation addressed to the sources of his deviant behavior." [19] While the right to rehabilitation for prisoners has by no means been generally accepted, at least some courts are beginning to require that the criminal justice system provide necessary rehabilitation services either under a due process or an Eighth Amendment rationale.

In *Newman v. Alabama*,[20] for example, state prisoners claimed that they were deprived of adequate medical treatment in violation of their rights guaranteed under the Eighth and Fourteenth Amendments to the United States Constitution. The court agreed and held that the failure of the Board of Corrections to provide sufficient medical facilities and staff to afford inmates basic elements of adequate medical care constituted willful and intentional violation of prisoners' constitutional rights. On the issue of whether *mental*-health standards were also an appropriate topic for court examination, the court ruled that the adequacy of care was to include both physical medical services and mental-health services. As the court specifically noted:

"The fate of those many prisoners who are mentally ill or retarded deserves special mention. Mental illness and mental retardation are the most prevalent medical problems in the Alabama prison system. . . . To diagnose and treat these almost 2400 inmates, the Board of Corrections employes one clinical psychologist, who works one afternoon each week. . . . There are no psychiatrists, social workers, or counsellors on the staff . . . [T]he large majority of mentally disturbed prisoners receive no treatment whatsoever. It is tautological that such care is constitutionally inadequate." [21]

The *Newman* case could have a major impact on correctional systems in this country. A major survey indicated that 160 correctional institutions, housing almost 150,000 inmates, employed only 14 full-time psychiatrists and 82 full-time psychologists; only six of these facilities provided a full range of programs.[22] These statistics dramatize the overwhelming inadequacy of diagnostic and treatment facilities within correctional institutions. The right to habilitation and treatment for mentally retarded prisoners articulated in *Newman* is obviously denied to all but a handful at present. It remains to be seen how quickly other courts will act to enforce this right.

NOTES

1. Brown & Courtless, "The Mentally Retarded in Penal and Correctional Institutions," 124 *Am J. Psychiatry* 1164, 1166 (1968).
2. *See* Allen, "The Retarded Offender: Unrecognized in Court and Untreated in Prison," 32 *Fed. Probation* 3, 22-24 (Sept. 1968).
3. The President's Panel on Mental Retardation, *Report of the Task Force on Law* (1963) [hereinafter "President's Panel"]. This chapter relies heavily upon the reasoning and recommendations of this report.
4. *Reck v. Pate,* 367 U.S. 433 (1961); *Culombe v. Connecticut,* 367 U.S. 568 (1961); *Fikes v. Alabama,* 352 U.S. 191 (1957).
5. President's Panel, *supra* note 3, at 32-34.
6. *See Commonwealth v. Daniels,* 321 N.E.2d 822, *especially* 826-828 (Mass. 1975).
7. President's Panel, *supra,* note 3, at 34. The fact that a mentally retarded defendant remains silent when accused of a crime may also be introduced as evidence by the prosecution in some jurisdictions as a tacit confession of guilt. Certainly for mentally retarded persons no such inference is justified. The silence is just as likely to relate to an inability to

understand what is being said or a lack of verbal facility to make an appropriate reply as it is to reflect guilt or innocence.

8. *United States v. Masthers,* No. 74-1602 (D.C. Cir., April 14, 1976).
9. *Id.* at 11-12.
10. *Id.* at 2 (concurrence).
11. 406 U.S. 715 (1972).
12. *Id.* at 738 (footnote omitted).
13. ALI Model Penal Code §4.06 (Proposed Official Draft 1962).
14. *Id.* §4.01.
15. 471 F.2d 969 (D.C. Cir. 1972).
16. *Id.* at 1002.
17. Brown & Courtless, *supra* note 1, at 1167.
18. Rowan, "Corrections," in *The Mentally Retarded Citizen and the Law* (M. Kindred et al. eds. 1976).
19. President's Panel, *supra* note 3, at 39.
20. 349 F. Supp. 278 (M.D. Ala. 1972), *aff'd,* 503 F.2d 1320 (5th Cir. 1974), *cert. denied,* 421 U.S. 948 (1975).
21. *Id.* at 284 (footnotes omitted).
22. Brown & Courtless, *supra* note 1, at 1167.

VI

The Right to a Legal Advocate

Do mentally retarded persons have a right to legal-advocacy services?

Yes. Without the services of legal advocates, many mentally retarded persons would be unable to assert effectively some or all of the legal rights described in the preceding pages. Recognizing this, both courts and state legislatures have acknowledged that mentally retarded persons have a right to effective legal advocates. In *Wyatt v. Stickney,* for example, the Federal district court appointed a seven-member "human rights committee" for Partlow State School. The human rights committee was charged with reviewing "all research proposals and all habilitation programs to insure that the dignity and human rights of residents are preserved" and with advising and assisting "residents who allege that their legal rights have been infringed or that the Mental Health Board has failed to comply with judicially ordered guidelines." [1] In a separate proceeding in which involuntary sterilizations were ruled unconstitutional and protective standards were established for "voluntary" sterilization of mentally retarded residents, the district court required that residents be provided with counsel in all proceedings concerning sterilization. [2] In another landmark case concerning civil commitment of mentally retarded children, the

149

U.S. Court of Appeals for the Tenth Circuit in *Heryford v. Parker* [3] held that under the due process clause of the Fourteenth Amendment a mentally deficient youngster was entitled to legal counsel in a judicial proceeding initiated by the mother and leading to confinement in a state institution. Three other Federal courts have recently reached the same conclusion. [4]

Recognizing the absolute necessity of competent legal advocacy yet also realizing how few lawyers there are at present with expertise and interest in the problems of mentally retarded persons, a number of state legislatures have established an advocacy agency by statute. One of the first was the New York Mental Health Information Service, established in 1965. During a substantial revision of the state's mental-hygiene law, effective in 1973, the client population of the Mental Health Information Service was expanded to include mentally retarded persons. [5] The New York Mental Health Information Service is charged with the protective duties to inform institutional residents and interested parties of the residents' rights and to provide service and assistance to residents and their families. [6] Under recent legislation in Ohio, an Ohio Legal Rights Service for the Mentally Retarded has been established and charged with representing mentally retarded persons both in and after commitment to institutions and with respect to the full range of their rights as citizens in the community. [7] The Mental Health Division of the New Jersey Public Advocate has similar responsibilities. [8]

Finally, Title II of the 1975 Federal Developmentally Disabled Assistance and Bill of Rights Act requires that all states receiving Federal formula grants for assistance to the developmentally disabled:

"[P]rovide the Secretary satisfactory assurances that not later than [October 1, 1977] (1) the State will have in effect a system to protect and advocate the rights of persons with developmental disabilities, and (2) such system will (A) have the authority to pursue legal, administrative, and other appropriate remedies to insure the protection of the rights of such persons who are receiving treatment, services, or habilitation within the State, and (B) be independent of any State agency which provides treatment, services, or habilitation to persons with developmental disabilities." [9]

What are the different forms of legal advocacy which may be used to assist mentally retarded persons?

First of all, it is necessary to clarify the distinction between legal advocacy and other forms of advocacy in general. Advocacy in general includes any activity which involves a person acting on his own behalf or on the behalf of another to secure responses to perceived needs. As defined by a leading authority, Dr. Wolf Wolfensberger, citizen advocacy involves "a mature, competent citizen volunteer representing, as if they were his own, the interests of another citizen who is impaired in his instrumental [problem solving] competency or who has major expressive [emotional] needs which are unmet and which are likely to remain unmet without special intervention." [10]

When a person attempts to secure the rights of mentally retarded persons by effecting legislation, by altering administrative rules or by litigation in court, such a person is engaging in *legal* advocacy, whether or not he or she is a lawyer. Obviously, however, there are certain legal-advocacy tasks—e.g., representing a client in a court civil commitment proceeding—which can only be performed by a lawyer duly admitted to the state bar.

Among advocacy roles most commonly assumed by attorneys on behalf of mentally retarded persons, there is a basic distinction between law-reform advocacy—

directed toward the broad recognition of basic legal rights for the entire class of mentally retarded persons —and case advocacy, which involves representation of a specific individual in a particular dispute.

At the moment, a number of different forms of legal advocacy are being tested around the country. Questions include whether attorneys should be selected to represent mentally retarded persons on a case-by-case basis. If so, should they come from a community pool composed of lawyers who have demonstrated interest and competence in the area, or should they be drawn from the legal community at large? Or should there be an agency—such as the New York Mental Health Information Service or the Ohio Legal Rights Service for the Mentally Retarded—employing full-time specialized personnel? Should such an agency be statewide or local? And should it be responsible to the state's mental-health department or to the judiciary or be established in such a way as to be fully independent? [11]

NOTES

1. *Wyatt v. Stickney*, 344 F. Supp. 387, 392 (M.D. Ala. 1972), *aff'd in part, remanded in part sub nom. Wyatt v. Aderholt*, 503 F.2d 1305 (5th Cir. 1974)
2. *Wyatt v. Aderholt*, 368 F. Supp. 1383, 1385 (M.D. Ala. 1974).
3. 396 F.2d 393 (10th Cir. 1968).
4. *Saville v. Treadway*, Civil Action No. Nashville 6969 (M.D. Tenn., Mar. 8, 1974) (consent decree); *Bartley v. Kremens*, 402 F. Supp. 1039 (E.D. Pa. 1975), *stay granted*, 96 S.Ct. 1457 (March 22, 1976); *J.L. v. Parham*, —— F. Supp. ——, No. 75-163 M.A.C. (M.D. Ga. 1976), *stay granted*, 96 S.Ct. 1503 (1976).
5. N.Y. Mental Hygiene Law §29.09 (McKinney Supp. 1975-76).
6. *Id.*

7. Ohio Rev. Code Ann. §§5119.85-.89 (Page Supp. 1974).
8. Department of the Public Advocate Act of 1974, N.J. Stat. Ann. §§ 52:27E-1, 52:27E-21 (Supp. 1975-76).
9. Pub. L. No. 94-103, 89 Stat. 486, §203 (Oct. 4, 1975), *to be codified at* 42 U.S.C. §6012.
10. W. Wolfensberger, *Citizen's Advocacy for the Handicapped, Impaired and Disadvantaged: An Overview* 12 (1972).
11. *See generally* Cohen, "Advocacy" in *The Mentally Retarded Citizen and the Law* (Kindred et al. eds. 1976).

APPENDICES

Appendix A

GLOSSARY OF LEGAL TERMS

advocate—An individual, whether a professional employed by a private or public agency or a volunteer (a citizen advocate), who acts on behalf of a mentally retarded person to secure both the services that the person requires and the exercise of his full human and legal rights.

amicus curiae—An individual or organization, neither plaintiff nor defendant, which, because of expertise or interest, is allowed to become involved in the case as "friend of the court." The involvement usually consists of submitting to the court a brief containing supporting legal arguments. Under extraordinary circumstances, the right actually to participate in the case and to present evidence and cross-examine witnesses can be granted.

appeal—The process whereby a court of appeals reviews the record of written materials from a trial-court proceeding to determine if errors were made which might lead to a reversal of the trial court's decision. If substantial errors are not found, the trial court's decision will be affirmed.

cause of action—A cause of action is the occurrence which has resulted in injury to one of a plaintiff's legally protected interests. A case is made up on one or more causes of action.

civil case or suit—A case brought by one or more individuals to seek redress of some legal injury (or aspect of an injury) for which there are civil (noncriminal) remedies.

class action—A case brought on behalf of the plaintiffs who are actually named in the suit and of all other persons similarly situated, to vindicate their legally protected interests.

complaint—A legal document submitted to the court by potential plaintiffs in which they inform the court and the defendants that they are bringing a lawsuit and set out the underlying causes of action.

consent decree or consent agreement—An out-of-court agreement reached by the parties to a suit, which may be formally approved by the court.

constitutional right—A legal right which is based on the United States Constitution or on a state constitution. Equal protection and due process of law are constitutional rights.

court systems—There are two court structures in the United States: the Federal courts (consisting mainly of Federal district courts where cases are tried, the U.S. Courts of Appeal for the eleven circuits or areas of the country and the U.S. Supreme Court) and the state courts (consisting of trial-level courts, called by various names, and one or two levels of appeals courts, depending on the size of the state and its caseload). Decisions by the highest court in a state are reviewable by the U.S. Supreme Court.

criminal suit—A case brought by a public prosecutor against someone who is alleged to have committed a wrong for which there are statutory criminal penalties.

damages—Money awarded by a court to someone who has been injured (the plaintiff) and which must be paid by the one who is responsible for the injury (the defendant). *Normal* damages are awarded when the injury is judged to be slight; *compensatory damages* are awarded to repay or compensate the injured person for the injury incurred, such as for medical expenses, for pain and suffering and for mental anguish. *Punitive damages* are awarded when the injury is judged to have been committed maliciously or in wanton disregard of the injured plaintiff's interests.

declaratory relief—A remedy granted by a court where the court declares or finds that plaintiffs have certain rights. A request for declaratory relief is usually coupled with a request for injunctive relief where the court orders defendants to take or refrain from taking certain actions.

defendant—The person against whom an action is brought because he is allegedly responsible for violation of one or more of a plaintiff's legally protected interests.

defense—A reason cited by a defendant why a complaint against him is without merit or why he is not responsible for the injury or violation of rights as alleged by the plaintiff. A defense might be that his actions were privileged or that the plaintiff consented to the action or even that procedural rules for bringing the suit against him were not properly followed.

discovery—The process by which one party to a civil suit can find out about matters which are relevant to his case, including information about what evidence the other side has, what witnesses will be called and so on. There are several discovery devices for obtaining information: depositions and interrogatories to obtain testimony, requests for documents or other tangibles and requests for physical or mental examinations.

due process of law—A right to have any law applied reasonably and with sufficient safeguards, such as hearings and notice to insure that an individual is dealt with fairly. Due process is guaranteed under the Fifth and Fourteenth Amendments to the U.S. Constitution.

equal protection of law—A right not to be discriminated against for any unjustifiable reason, such as race or handicap. Equal protection is guaranteed under the Fourteenth Amendment.

expert witness—A person called to testify because he has a recognized competence in an area.

Federal courts—See "court systems" above.

guardian—An individual who has legal control and management of the person, or of the property or estate, or of both the person and the property of another. A *natural guardian* is a parent lawfully in control of the person of his minor child; natural guardianship terminates when the child attains his majority. A *legal guardian* is one appointed by a court. A *guardian of the person* is one appointed to see that the mentally retarded person has proper care and protective supervision in keeping with his needs. A *guardian of the property or estate* is one appointed to see that the financial affairs of the mentally retarded person are handled in his best interests. A *guardian ad litem* is one appointed to represent a metally retarded person in a particular legal proceeding, without control over either his person or his estate. A *public guardian* is a public official empowered to accept court appointment as a legal guardian. A *testamentary guardian* is one designated by the last will and testament of a natural guardian.

injunctive relief—A remedy granted by the court forbidding or requiring some action by the defendant. Injunctive relief includes temporary restraining orders and preliminary and final injunctions.

judgment—An order by a judge after a verdict has been reached which sets out what relief is to be granted to the winning side.

legal incompetence—The legal determination that a mentally handicapped person is unable to exercise his full civil and legal rights and that a *guardian* is required.

motions—A request to the court to take some action or to request the opposing side to take some action relating to a case. Motions generally relate to pretrial or trial procedures, such as a *motion for a more definitive statement,* a *motion to dismiss* the case, etc.

next friend—A person who represents the interests of a minor or an incompetent in a legal action. A next friend or *guardian ad litem* is usually a parent or guardian but may be an important person in the community or an interested organization.

plaintiff—A person who brings a suit in court in the belief that one or more of his legal rights have been violated or that he has suffered legal injury.

pleadings—A term which encompasses all of the preliminary steps of complaint-answer-replies used to narrow a case down to the basic issues of law and fact. It is also used more specifically to refer to a plaintiff setting forth his cause of action and the relief which he is requesting from the court.

precedent—A decision by a judge or court which serves as a rule or guide to support other judges in deciding future cases involving similar or analogous legal questions.

private action—A case brought on behalf of one or more individuals to vindicate violation of their legally protected interest. As distinguished from a class action, where the relief will apply to all persons similarly situated or within the class represented by the plaintiffs, any relief granted in a private action applies only to those plaintiffs actually before the court.

procedural right—A right relating to the process of enforcing substantive rights or to obtaining relief, such as the right to a hearing, the right to present evidence in one's defense or the right to counsel.

relief—A remedy for some legal wrong. Relief is requested by a plaintiff to be granted by a court against a defendant.

settlement—An out-of-court agreement among parties to a suit, which resolves some or all of the issues involved in a case.

state courts—See "court systems" above.

statutory right—A right based on a statute or law passed by a unit of Federal, state or local government.

substantive right—An essential right such as the right to free speech and religion or to be free from involuntary servitude, usually found in the Bill of Rights.

surrogate—An individual who functions in lieu of a resident's parents or family.

test case—A case brought to establish a legal principle as well as to vindicate rights of the parties involved in the specific case. Once principles are established in one court, they can be cited as precedent for decisions by other judges or other courts.

tort—A civil wrong for which a private individual may recover money damages. Torts include, for example, assault and battery, intentional infliction of mental distress, false imprisonment and invasion of privacy.

verdict—A decision by a judge or jury in favor on one side or the other in a case.

GLOSSARY OF MENTAL RETARDATION TERMS

adaptive behavior—How well the individual solves problems in his environment and how well he adapts to the behavioral expectations and standards of society.

autism—A condition observed in young children, characterized by severe withdrawal and inappropriate response to external stimulation.

cerebral palsy—A condition caused by injury to the nervous tissues in the cranial cavity. Mental retardation may or may not accompany the resulting motor dysfunction, although it is estimated that 50 to 75 percent of those with cerebral palsy are mentally retarded as well.

functional retardation—Describes the child of normal brain who functions poorly due to cultural or emotional deprivation. Given the right kind and amount of stimulus, such a child may improve immeasurably.

habilitation—Improvement in a skill or level of adjustment, as with respect to an increase in the ability to maintain satisfactory employment.

intelligence—Although there is no universally agreed-upon definition of intelligence, it may be defined generally as problem-solving ability, ability to adapt approximately to environmental demands and ability to apprehend abstract interrelationships. (For specific purposes, intelligence is often defined in a more restricted sense.)

intelligence quotient (I.Q.)—An intelligence-test score; also the relationship between chronological age and mental age.

$$\text{I.Q.} = \frac{\text{M.A.}}{\text{C.A.}} \times 100$$

mental deficiency—A synonym for mental retardation. Sometimes used in a more restricted sense to refer to those whose mental retardation is attributable to structural defect.

mental retardation—Refers to significantly subaverage general intellectual functioning existing concurrently with deficits in adaptive behavior and manifested during the developmental period. The correlation between these levels of retardation and performance on the revised Stanford-Binet I.Q. test has been given as follows:

Current Retardation Term	Revised Stanford-Binet I.Q.
Mild	68-52
Moderate	51-36
Severe	35-20
Profound	below 20

normalization principle—The principle of letting the mentally retarded "obtain an existence as close to the normal as possible," making available to them "patterns and conditions of everyday life which are as close as possible to the norms and patterns of the mainstream of society."

rehabilitation—Restoration of a skill or restoration of efficiency to a level compatible with partial or complete vocational and social independence.

resident—The general term used to refer to mentally retarded persons who receive services from a residential facility.

sheltered workshop—A facility which provides occupational training and/or protective employment for mentally retarded persons and/or persons with other handicapping conditions.

special class—A class, usually in a school setting, that provides special instruction for mentally retarded children as well as for other types of students with special needs.

Appendix B

SELECT BIBLIOGRAPHY

Articles and Policy Statements

American Association on Mental Deficiency, "Policy Statement Supplement," 13 Mental Retardation C-1-15 (April 1975).

American Association on Mental Deficiency, "Policy Statement Supplement," 11 Mental Retardation 56-62 (October 1973).

Friedman & Beck, "Mental Retardation and the Law: A Comprehensive Summary of the Status of Current Court Cases" (Sept. 1975).

Haggerty, Kane and Udall, "Essay on the Legal Rights of the Mentally Retarded," 6 Family Law Quarterly 59 (1972).

National Association for Retarded Citizens, Policy Statements on Residential Services (Oct. 19, 1968).

Murdock, "Civil Rights of the Mentally Retarded: Some Critical Issues," 7 Family Law Quarterly 1, (1973); 48 Notre Dame Lawyer 133 (1972).

Symposium: The Legal Rights of the Mentally Retarded, 23 Syracruse L. Rev. 991 (1972).

Books and Monographs

ACTION AGAINST MENTAL DISABILITY: THE

REPORT OF THE PRESIDENT'S TASK FORCE ON THE MENTALLY HANDICAPPED (Sept. 1970).

R.C. Allen, LEGAL RIGHTS OF THE DISABLED AND DISADVANTAGED (1969).

S. Brakel and R. Rock, THE MENTALLY DISABLED AND THE LAW (1971).

B. Ennis and P. Friedman (eds.), LEGAL RIGHTS OF THE MENTALLY HANDICAPPED (1974).

M. Kindred, J. Cohen, D. Penrod, and T. Schaffer (eds.), THE MENTALLY RETARDED CITIZEN AND THE LAW (1976).

Mental Health Law Project, BASIC RIGHTS OF THE MENTALLY HANDICAPPED (1973).

NARC Insurance Committee, HOW TO PROVIDE FOR THEIR FUTURE (Rev. ed. 1975).

F. Ogg, SECURING THE LEGAL RIGHTS OF RE-TARDED PERSONS (1973).

J. Paul, R. Wiegerink and G. Neufeld (eds.) ADVO-CACY: A ROLE FOR DEVELOPMENTAL DIS-ABILITIES COUNCILS (1975).

Pennsylvania Association for Retarded Citizens, A HANDBOOK ON THE LEGAL RIGHTS OF THE MENTALLY RETARDED (1974).

The President's Committee on Mental Retardation Legal Rights Work Group, COMPENDIUM OF CLASS ACTION LAWSUITS RELATED TO THE LEGAL RIGHTS OF THE MENTALLY RETARDED (1973).

The President's Committee on Mental Retardation, MR 70: THE DECISIVE DECADE (1971).

The President's Committee on Mental Retardation, MR 71: ENTERING THE ERA OF HUMAN ECOLOGY (1972).

The President's Committee on Mental Retardation, MENTAL RETARDATION: CENTURY OF DE-CISION (1976).

The President's Committee on Mental Retardation, MENTAL RETARDATION . . . THE KNOWN AND THE UNKNOWN (1975).

The President's Committee on Mental Retardation, SILENT MINORITY (1973).

U.S. Dept. of HEW, SOCIAL SECURITY HANDBOOK (Fifth ed.).

W. Wolfensberger, THE PRINCIPLE OF NORMALIZATION IN HUMAN SERVICES (1972).

Appendix C

LIST OF RESOURCE ORGANIZATIONS

NATIONAL

American Association on Mental Deficiency
5201 Connecticut Avenue, N.W.
Washington, D.C. 20015

American Bar Association
Commission on the Mentally Disabled
1800 M Street, N.W.
Washington, D.C. 20036

ACLU Juvenile Rights Project
22 East 40th Street
New York, New York 10016

Center on Human Policy
Division of Special Education & Rehabilitation
Syracuse University
Syracuse, New York 13210

Child Welfare League of America, Inc.
44 East 23rd Street
New York, New York 10010

Children's Defense Fund
1520 New Hampshire Ave. N.W.
Washington, D.C. 20036

Civil Rights Division
United States Department of Justice

1121 Vermont Ave. N.W.
Washington, D.C. 20005

The Council for Exceptional Children
900 Jefferson Plaza
1411 Jefferson Davis Highway
Arlington, Virginia 22202

Institute for the Study of Mental Retardation
and Related Disabilities
130 South First
University of Michigan
Ann Arbor, Michigan 48108

International League of Societies for the
Mentally Handicapped
Rue Forestiere 12
Brussels, BELGIUM

Joseph P. Kennedy, Jr. Foundation
1701 K Street, N.W.
Washington, D.C. 20006

Mental Health Law Project
1220 19th St. N.W.
Washington, D.C. 20036

National Association of Coordinators of
State Programs for the Mentally Retarded
2001 Jefferson Davis Highway
Arlington, Virginia 22202

The National Association for Retarded Citizens
2709 Avenue E East
Arlington, Texas 76010

National Center for Law and the Handicapped
1238 North Eddy Street
South Bend, Indiana 46617

National Legal Aid & Defender Association
1155 East 60th Street
Chicago, Illinois 60637

National Prison Project
ACLU
1346 Connecticut Avenue, N.W.
Washington, D.C. 20036

President's Committee on Mental Retardation
Regional Office Building #3
7th & D Streets, S.W.
Room 2614
Washington, D.C. 20201

Public Information & Education
ENCOR
116 South 42nd Street
Omaha, Nebraska 68131

Youth Law Center
693 Mission Street
San Francisco, California 94105

STATE

Legal Aid Society of Minneapolis
501 Park Avenue
Minneapolis, Minnesota 55415

Department of the Public Advocate
State of New Jersey
10-12 North Stockton Street
Trenton, New Jersey 08625

Federation of Parents Organizations
   for the New York State Mental Institutions
162 West 56th Street
New York, New York 10019

Mental Health Information Service
27 Madison Avenue
New York, New York 10010

Mental Health Law Project (New York Office)
84 Fifth Avenue
New York, New York 10011

Institutional Legal Services
5308 Ballard Avenue
Seattle, Washington 98107

Milwaukee Legal Services
1006 South 16th Street
Milwaukee, Wisconsin 53204

LIST OF STATE CHAPTERS OF THE NATIONAL ASSOCIATION FOR RETARDED CITIZENS

ALABAMA—4301 Norman Bridge Rd., Montgomery 36105

ALASKA—Star Route A, Box 23H, Anchorage 99507

ARIZONA—5610 S. Central, Phoenix 75040

ARKANSAS—University Shopping Center, Little Rock 72204

CALIFORNIA—1225 Eighth St., Suite 312, Sacramento 95314

COLORADO—643 S. Broadway, Denver 80209

CONNECTICUT—410 Asylum St., Hartford 06103

DELAWARE—Box 1896, Wilmington 19899

DISTRICT OF COLUMBIA—405 Riggs Rd., N.E., Washington, D.C. 20011

FLORIDA—P.O. Box 1542, Tallahassee 32302

GEORGIA—1575 Phoenix Blvd, Suite 8, Atlanta 30349

HAWAII—245 N. Kukui St., Honolulu 96817

IDAHO—P.O. Box 816, Boise 83701

ILLINOIS—#6 N. Michigan Ave., Chicago 60602

INDIANA—752 E. Market St., Indianapolis 46202

IOWA—1707 High St., Des Moines 50309

KANSAS—6100 Martway, Suite 1, Mission 66202

KENTUCKY—P.O. Box 275, Frankfort 40601

LOUISIANA—7465 Exchange Pl., Baton Rouge 70806

MAINE—269½ Water St., Augusta 04330

MARYLAND—55 Gwynns Mill Ct., Owings Mills 21117

MASSACHUSETTS—381 Elliot St., Newton Upper Falls 02164

MICHIGAN—416 Michigan National Tower, Lansing 48933

MINNESOTA—3225 Lyndale Ave., Minneapolis 55408

MISSISSIPPI—Box 1363, Jackson 39205

MISSOURI—230 W. Dunklin, Jefferson City 65101

MONTANA—P.O. Box 625, Helena 59601

NEBRASKA—620 N. 48th S-318, Lincoln, 68504

NEVADA—1800 E. Sahara Ave., Suite 102, Las Vegas 89104

NEW HAMPSHIRE—52 Pleasant St., Concord 03301

NEW JERSEY—97 Bayard St., New Brunswick 08901

NEW MEXICO—8200½ Menaul Blvd. NE, Suite 3, Albuquerque 87110

NORTH CAROLINA—P.O. Box 18551, Raleigh 27609

NORTH DAKOTA—207 E. Broadway, Bismarck 58501

OHIO—61 E. Gay St., Columbus 43215

OKLAHOMA—P.O. Box 14250, Oklahoma City 73114

OREGON—3085 River Rd. N., Salem 97303

PENNSYLVANIA—1500 N. Second, Harrisburg 17102

RHODE ISLAND—Snow Bldg, 2845 Post Rd, Warwick 02886

SOUTH CAROLINA—P.O. Box 1564, Columbia 29202

SOUTH DAKOTA—P.O. Box 502, 111 W. Capitol, Pierre 57501

TENNESSEE—2121 Belcourt Ave., Nashville 37212

TEXAS—833 W. Houston, Austin 78756

UTAH—2952 S. 7th East, Salt Lake City 84106

VERMONT—323 Pearl St., Burlington 05401

VIRGINIA—827 E. Main St., Suite 1801, Richmond 23219

WASHINGTON—213½ E. 4th, Suite 10, Olympia 98501

WEST VIRGINIA—Union Trust Bldg. Rm 614, Parkersburg 26101

WISCONSIN—351 W. Washington Ave., Madison 53703

WYOMING—Box C, Buffalo 82834

'Appendix D

UNITED NATIONS
GENERAL ASSEMBLY

Declaration on the Rights of
Mentally Retarded Persons

Adopted 20 December 1971

The General Assembly,

Mindful of the pledge of the States Members of the United Nations under the Charter to take joint and separate action in co-operation with the Organization to promote higher standards of living, full employment and conditions of economic and social progress and development,

Reaffirming faith in human rights and fundamental freedoms and in the principles of peace, of the dignity and worth of the human person and of social justice proclaimed in the Charter,

Recalling the principles of the Universal Declaration of Human Rights, the International Covenants on Human Rights,[1] the Declaration of the Rights of the Child [2] and the standards already set for social progress in the constitutions, conventions, recommendations and resolutions of the International Labour Oragnization, the United Nations Educational, Scientific and Cultural Organization, the World Health Organization, the United Nations Children's Fund and of other organizations concerned,

Emphasizing that the Declaration on Social Progress and Development [8] has proclaimed the necessity of protecting the rights and assuring the welfare and rehabilitation of the physically and mentally disadvantaged.

Bearing in mind the necessity of assisting mentally retarded persons to develop their abilities in various fields of activities and of promoting their integration as far as possible in normal life,

Aware that certain countries, at their present stage of development, can devote only limited efforts to this end,

Proclaims this Declaration on the Rights of Mentally Retarded Persons and calls for national and international action to ensure that it will be used as a common basis and frame of reference for the protection of these rights:

1. The mentally retarded person has, to the maximum degree of feasibility, the same rights as other human beings.

2. The mentally retarded person has a right to proper medical care and physical therapy and to such education, training, rehabilitation and guidance as will enable him to develop his ability and maximum potential.

3. The mentally retarded person has a right to economic security and to a decent standard of living. He has a right to perform productive work or to engage in any other meaningful occupation to the fullest possible extent of his capabilities.

4. Whenever possible, the mentally retarded person should live with his own family or with foster parents and participate in different forms of community life. The family with which he lives should receive assistance. If care in an institution becomes necessary, it should be provided in surroundings and other circumstances as close as possible to those of normal life.

5. The mentally retarded person has a right to a qualified guardian when this is required to protect his personal well-being and interests.

6. The mentally retarded person has a right to protection from exploitation, abuse and degrading treatment. If prosecuted for any offense, he shall have a right to due process of law with full recognition being given to his degree of mental responsibility.

7. Whenever mentally retarded persons are unable, because of the severity of their handicap, to exercise all their rights in a meaningful way or it should become necessary to restrict or deny some or all of these rights, the procedure used for that restriction or denial of rights must contain proper legal safeguards against every form of abuse. This procedure must be based on an evaluation of the social capability of the mentally retarded person by qualified experts and must be subject to periodic review and to the right of appeal to higher authorities.

2027th plenary meeting,
20 December 1971.

[1] Resolution 2200 A (XXI).
[2] Resolution 1386 (XIV).
[3] Resolution 2542 (XXIV).

Appendix E

RIGHTS OF MENTALLY RETARDED PERSONS:

An Official Statement of the American
Association on Mental Deficiency

PREFACE

The American Association on Mental Deficiency supports the "Declaration of General and Special Rights of the Mentally Retarded" as adopted by the International League of Societies for the Mentally Handicapped, but recognizes the need to make statements more specific in nature and to make recommendations for action. Accordingly, the following document represents the Association's position on these matters, and is the Association's basic statement of policy. Future activities of the Association will be guided by this document, and will be directed to the fulfillment of its aims, in manners consistent with professional responsibility and professional opinion.

Professionals in the field, individually and in concert, should assert leadership in the protection of these rights, in assuring their exercise and enjoyment by retarded citizens, and in the implementation of these rights to provide for more satisfying circumstances of life for retarded persons.

The Association will pursue these goals through its regional and national organizations, through its publications, and through its membership in other groups.

The Association will also help to design, to promulgate, and to implement programs of preparation for professionals, paraprofessionals, and nonprofessionals that will facilitate their safeguarding and implementation of the rights of retarded persons as expressed in this statement. The Association will assist in the drafting of model legislation; will, on request, comment on and assist in the development of specific proposals for legislation that would affect retarded persons; and will participate, as appropriate, in legal proceedings of significant import and appropriate focus.

Professionals should bear in mind the statements in this document when preparing both general and individual programs for retarded persons, when designing facilities and organizing services for retarded persons, when taking part in the legislative process, when taking part in the judicial process, when considering the allocation of fiscal and other resources, when hiring workers, when seeking employment, when teaching, when conducting research, and most of all, when participating directly in the treatment, training, and habilitation of retarded persons. When a professional sees that retarded individuals are being dealt with in a manner inconsistent with the principles expressed in this document, then that professional person should act in a conscientious manner to remedy the situation immediately, through individual or group action, and by formal or informal process. This may be accomplished through job action, through administrative action, through legislative action, through judicial action, or through whatever public and private means are available, moral, ethical, and legal. The Association pledges to support such efforts in order to ensure the fullest exercise of professional skills and judgment on behalf of retarded persons. Association and individual action should be taken whenever an issue arises that affects the community of interests of retarded persons, whether that effect is direct or indirect.

Mentally retarded citizens are entitled to enjoy and to exercise the same rights as are available to nonretarded citizens, to the limits of their ability to do so. As handicapped citizens, they are also entitled to specific extensions of, and additions to, these basic rights, in order to allow their free exercise and enjoyment. When an individual retarded citizen is unable to enjoy and exercise his or her rights, it is the obligation of the society to intervene so as to safeguard these rights, and to act humanely and conscientiously on that person's behalf.

BASIC RIGHTS

I. The basic rights that a retarded person shares with his or her nonretarded peers include, but are not limited to, those implied in "life, liberty, and the pursuit of happiness," and those specified in detail in the various documents that provide the basis for governing democratic nations. Specific rights of mentally retarded persons include, but are not limited to:

A. The right to freedom of choice within the individual's capacity to make decisions and within the limitations imposed on all persons.

B. The right to live in the least restrictive individually appropriate environment.

Nonretarded adults have considerable latitude to control their own lives, particularly in terms of choosing place of employment and place of residence. Insofar as he or she is able to make these choices, a retarded adult should have the same freedom of choice. A classification of mental retardation is not, of itself, sufficient cause to restrict an individual's freedom of movement.

C. The right to gainful employment, and to a fair day's pay for a fair day's labor.

A retarded individual should be allowed to work at whatever job he or she is capable of performing and should be paid at a level reflecting his or her productivity. If a retarded person cannot work in the community at large, and is to be appropriately employed at the maintenance of the public or private institution at which he resides, then he also should be paid according to his level of productivity, and should receive appropriate fringe benefits. In no event should a retarded individual be retained at any facility solely because his or her presence enables the institution to maintain itself.

D. The right to be part of a family.

A retarded individual should not be summarily excised from his family, and should be permitted and encouraged to be with them whenever his developmental needs can be met satisfactorily in this manner. If he or she is an institutional resident, family visits should be encouraged, except when such contact may be detrimental to the individual's well-being.

E. The right to marry and have a family of his or her own.

Any retarded citizen who can be effectively self-supporting, and who can be reasonably expected to discharge effectively the obligations of marriage and parenthood, should be permitted to marry and to raise a family; in no event, once a retarded person is married, should this marriage be annulled on the basis of the exclusive circumstance of mental retardation, nor should that person's right to bear and rear children be abridged. If a genetically transmitted condition exists, the retarded person should receive appropriate genetic counseling to ensure his understanding of the condition. If it should become evident that a retarded individual has become incapable of rearing his or her children, as may also occur with nonretarded parents, the same legal and professional procedures concerning parenthood that are applicable to families of nonretarded citizens should be applied to those of retarded citizens.

F. The right to freedom of movement, hence not to be interned without just cause and due process of law, including the right not to be permanently deprived of liberty by institutionalization in lieu of imprisonment.

If a retarded individual is brought to trial and ruled incompetent to defend himself, legal counsel must be provided, at public expense if necessary. A retarded person must not be remanded to any public institution interminably. When a retarded citizen has been judged to be incompetent to stand trial, that citizen must be provided an integrated, individualized, and comprehensive habilitative program. Regular judicial and programmatic review of an individual's program must be maintained.

G. The rights to speak openly and fully without fear of undue punishment, to privacy, to the practice of a religion, (or the practice of no religion), and to interact with peers.

A retarded individual should not be made to fear that interacting either exclusively with his or her retarded peers, or with members of society at large, will subject him or her to recrimination. Further, he or she must not be made to fear that complaint about or concern with the character of his or her public care will result in retribution. Every effort should be made for each retarded citizen to have time and space for his or her exclusive use.

SPECIFIC EXTENSIONS

II. Specific extensions of, and additions to, these basic rights, which are due mentally handicapped persons because of their special needs, include, but are not limited to:

A. The right to a publicly supported and administered comprehensive and integrated set of habilitative programs and services designed to minimize handicap or handicaps.

The retarded individual may reasonably expect a program of habilitation geared to his or her individual needs at public expense. This program of habilitation should recognize the individual's handicap(s), but should be geared to allowing that individual to function in a way as nearly as possible approximating the functioning of nonretarded citizens. Each individual, however severe his handicaps, should be helped to realize his maximum potential through an individualized habilitative program that takes maximum advantage of all relevant services, including social welfare services, medical services, housing services, vocational services, transportation services, legal services, and financial assistance services. The program should be subject to regular reevaluation and open review, and should be adapted to reflect the growth and learning of the retarded individual.

For those severely handicapped individuals who may never be able to function independently, it is the responsibility of the larger society to provide effective and humane supervised care using the full spectrum of resources essential to the person's optimal development in the least restrictive setting consistent with the individual's capacities and needs.

B. The right to a publicly supported and administered program of training and education including, but not restricted to, basic academic and interpersonal skills.

The society must make every effort to enable its retarded citizens, from childhood, to learn and use the skills that are necessary to function in the least restrictive setting possible and to function in the community at large with the least supervision that is appropriate. Among the skills that retarded persons should be afforded the opportunity to learn are self-help skills, money handling, use of transportation services, adaptive interpersonal behavior, reading, writing, the ability to take advantage of other services and sources of assistance in the community, and rewarding use of leisure time.

C. The right, beyond those implicit in the right to education described above, to a publicly administered and supported program of training toward the goal of maximum gainful employment, insofar as the individual is capable.

The public should provide a comprehensive set of appropriate programs of vocational training designed for retarded citizens. These may be provided through such situations as residential institutions, day care centers, sheltered workshops, vocational rehabilitation centers, or in apprenticeship programs in the larger community. To the extent possible, government at all levels should attempt to see that positions are available for retarded individuals upon completion of their training, either in publicly sponsored programs or in private employment. Governments also should encourage the employment of retarded workers, by eliminating legal and other artificial barriers to their obtaining jobs.

D. The right to protection against exploitation, demeaning treatment, or abuse.

Retarded individuals should not be exploited, either by those who have been entrusted with their care or by members of the society at large. (Such exploitation in the past has frequently resulted from the individual retarded person's inability either to perceive the exploitative aspect of a situation or to defend himself or herself against it.)

E. The right, when participating in research, to be safeguarded from violations of human dignity and to be protected from physical and psychological harm.

In securing that right, it is essential that research with retarded persons be carried out only with the informed consent of the subjects (or, in very special cases, of their legal guardians), that retarded persons be made aware of their right not to participate, and that such research as may be done with retarded persons adhere to recognized contemporary standards of ethics and scholarship.

Nonparticipation in research must never be followed by aversive consequences or the threat or implied threat of aversive consequences. Given the limited ability of many retarded persons to comprehend the nature and possible risks of a research program, it is necessary that particular care be taken to assure that research subjects are truly informed on what is required of them, what risks (and possible benefits) are involved, and what will be done with the data. Investigators have a responsibility to confine their research with retarded persons to those studies whose outcomes are likely to bear some ultimate benefit to retarded persons.

The rights of retarded persons with respect to participation in research should be monitored and secured by some third party or group, rather than being left to the discretionary interpretation of individual scientists.

F. The right, for a retarded individual who may not be able to act effectively in his or her own behalf, to have a responsible impartial guardian or advocate appointed by the society to protect and effect the exercise and enjoyment of these foregoing rights, insofar as this guardian, in accord with responsible professional opinion, determines that the retarded citizen is able to enjoy and exercise these rights.

A retarded individual frequently requires the good offices and efforts of nonretarded citizens in order to have his or her welfare safeguarded. In most instances, this fellow citizen will be a member of the retarded individual's family. Occasionally, however, it becomes necessary to have an unrelated citizen or agency act in the retarded person's behalf. The appointment of such a guardian is generally made by the courts; the guardian may be responsible both for the retarded person's estate and for his person. Such appointments should continue to be made by the courts, but only with competent professional advice. The guardian of a retarded individual should not be a public official responsible for the direct and immediate care and management of that particular person.

It is the responsibility of the guardian to determine, in a manner consistent with reliable contemporary knowledge, the extent to which the individual with whose care he or she is entrusted can function independently, to determine the extent of that person's ability to enjoy and exercise his or her rights, and to seek the exercise thereof.

Discus Books  **Distinguished Non-fiction**

Isaac Asimov
THE UNIVERSE
FROM FLAT EARTH TO QUASAR

27979 $1.95

Dr. Asimov leads a breathtaking voyage of discovery through time and space that makes even the most complex theoretical concepts comprehensible, and that furnishes the basic knowledge with which to understand coming developments.

ILLUSTRATED WITH PHOTOGRAPHS AND DRAWINGS

DISCUS BOOKS
DISTINGUISHED NON-FICTION

THEATER, FILM, AND TELEVISION

ACTORS TALK ABOUT ACTING Lewis Funke and John Booth, Eds.	15062	1.95
ACTION FOR CHILDREN'S TELEVISION	10090	1.25
ANTONIN ARTAUD Bettina L. Knapp	12062	1.65
A BOOK ON THE OPEN THEATER Robert Pasoli	12047	1.65
THE CONCISE ENCYCLOPEDIC GUIDE TO SHAKESPEARE Michael Martin and Richard Harrier, Eds.	16832	2.65
THE DISNEY VERSION Richard Schickel	08953	1.25
EDWARD ALBEE: A PLAYWRIGHT IN PROTEST Michael E. Rutenberg	11916	1.65
THE EMPTY SPACE Peter Brook	19802	1.65
EXPERIMENTAL THEATER James Roose-Evans	11981	1.65
FOUR CENTURIES OF SHAKESPEARIAN CRITICISM Frank Kermode, Ed.	20131	1.95
GUERILLA STREET THEATRE Henry Lesnick, Ed.	15198	2.45
THE HOLLYWOOD SCREENWRITERS Richard Corliss	12450	1.95
IN SEARCH OF LIGHT: THE BROADCASTS OF EDWARD R. MURROW Edward Bliss, Ed.	19372	1.95
INTERVIEWS WITH FILM DIRECTORS Andrew Sarris	21568	1.65
MOVIES FOR KIDS Edith Zornow and Ruth Goldstein	17012	1.65
PICTURE Lillian Ross	08839	1.25
THE LIVING THEATRE Pierre Biner	17640	1.65
PUBLIC DOMAIN Richard Schechner	12104	1.65
RADICAL THEATRE NOTEBOOK Arthur Sainer	22442	2.65

GENERAL NON-FICTION

ADDING A DIMENSION Isaac Asimov	22673	1.25
A TESTAMENT Frank Lloyd Wright	12039	1.65
AMBIGUOUS AFRICA Georges Balandier	25288	2.25
THE AMERICAN CHALLENGE J. J. Servan Schreiber	11965	1.65
AMERICA THE RAPED Gene Marine	09373	1.25
ARE YOU RUNNING WITH ME, JESUS? Malcolm Boyd	09993	1.25
THE AWAKENING OF INTELLIGENCE J. Krishnamurti	27342	2.65
BLACK HISTORY: LOST, STOLEN, OR STRAYED Otto Lindenmeyer	09167	1.25
THE BOOK OF IMAGINARY BEINGS Jorge Luis Borges	11080	1.45
BUILDING THE EARTH Pierre de Chardin	08938	1.25
CHEYENNE AUTUMN Mari Sandoz	09001	1.25
THE CHILD IN THE FAMILY Maria Montessori	28118	1.50
THE CHILDREN'S REPUBLIC Edward Mobius	21337	1.50
CHINA: SCIENCE WALKS ON TWO LEGS Science for the People	20123	1.75
CLASSICS REVISITED Kenneth Rexroth	08920	1.25
THE COMPLETE HOME MEDICAL ENCYCLOPEDIA Dr. Harold T. Hyman	15214	1.95

DISCUS BOOKS

DISTINGUISHED NON-FICTION

American Civil Liberties Union Handbooks on The Rights of Americans

THE RIGHTS OF CANDIDATES AND VOTERS
B. Newborne and A. Eisenberg   28159 1.50

THE RIGHTS OF MENTAL PATIENTS
Bruce Ennis and Loren Siegel   10652 1.25

THE RIGHTS OF THE POOR
Sylvia Law   28001 1.25

THE RIGHTS OF PRISONERS
David Rudovsky   07591   .95

THE RIGHTS OF SERVICEMEN
Robert S. Rivkin   28019 1.25

THE RIGHTS OF STUDENTS
Alan H. Levine with Eve Carey and Diane Divoky   05776   .95

THE RIGHTS OF SUSPECTS
Oliver Rosengart   28043 1.25

THE RIGHTS OF TEACHERS
David Rubin   25049 1.50

THE RIGHTS OF WOMEN
Susan Deller Ross   27953 1.75

THE RIGHTS OF REPORTERS
Joel M. Gora   21485 1.50

THE RIGHTS OF HOSPITAL PATIENTS
George J. Annas   22459 1.50

TH RIGHTS OF GAY PEOPLE E. Carrington
Boggan, Marilyn G. Haft, Charles Lister, John P. Rupp 24976 1.75

Wherever better paperbacks are sold, or direct from the
publisher. Include 25¢ per copy for mailing; allow three
weeks for delivery.

Avon Books, Mail Order Dept.,
250 West 55th Street, New York, N.Y. 10019

ACLU 6-76